THE BEST
IN TENT
CAMPING

OREGON

FIRST EDITION

PORTIONS OF THIS GUIDE FIRST APPEARED IN
THE BEST IN TENT CAMPING: WASHINGTON AND OREGON

THE BEST IN TENT CAMPING

A GUIDE FOR CAR CAMPERS WHO HATE RVs, CONCRETE SLABS, AND LOUD PORTABLE STEREOS

OREGON

FIRST EDITION

JEANNE LOUISE PYLE

MENASHA RIDGE PRESS

BIRMINGHAM, ALABAMA

Published by Menasha Ridge Press
Distributed by the Globe Pequot Press
First edition, first printing

Library of Congress Cataloging-in-Publication Data
Pyle, Jeanne L., 1954–
    The best in tent camping, Oregon: a guide for campers who hate RVs, concrete slabs,
and loud portable stereos / Jeanne L. Pyle.
p.cm.
        ISBN 0-89732-570-2
        1. Camping—Oregon—Guidebooks. 2. Camp sites, facilities, etc.—Oregon—Guide-
books.
3. Oregon—Guidebooks. I. Title.

        GV191,42.O7P95 2004
        796.54'09795—dc22   2004040339

Cover and text design by Ian Szymkowiak, Palace Press International, Inc.
Cover photo by Dennis Coello
Maps by Steve Jones

Menasha Ridge Press
P.O. Box 43673
Birmingham, Alabama 35243
www.menasharidge.com

TABLE OF CONTENTS

NORTHERN COAST 7

CENTRAL AND SOUTHERN COAST 23

NORTHERN CASCADES AND ENVIRONS 43

CENTRAL CASCADES AND ENVIRONS 75

MAP LEGEND

WHITE WOLF

Campground name
and location

Individual Tent and RV
campsites within
campground area

Table Rock

Other nearby
campgrounds

NATIONAL STATE
FOREST PARK

Public lands

64

Interstate
highways

19 219

U.S.
highways

Other roads

Unpaved or
gravel roads

Boardwalk

Political
boundary

Railroads

Hiking, biking,
or horse trail

Swift Creek

River or stream

Asheville

City
or town

N

Indicates North

Ward Lake

Ocean, lake,
or bay

Bridge or tunnel

Amphitheater

Falls or rapids

Equestrian site

Rest room

Water access

Gate

Trash disposal

HS Host site

Parking

Marina or boat ramp

Fire ring

Telephone

Laundry

Wheelchair access

Swimming

Picnic area

Sheltered
picnic area

Spring/Well

Dishwater disposal

Summit
or lookou

Bathhouse

Trailer dumpsite

No swimming

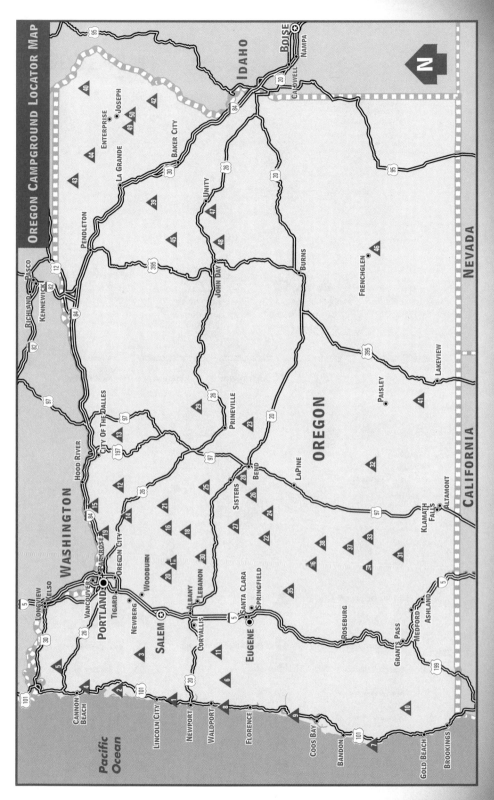

KEY TO OREGON CAMPGROUND LOCATOR MAP

NORTHERN COAST
1 BEVERLY BEACH STATE PARK
2 CAPE LOOKOUT STATE PARK
3 DOVRE, ELK BEND & THE NESTUCCA
   RIVER CAMPGROUNDS
4 OSWALD WEST STATE PARK
5 SADDLE MOUNTAIN STATE PARK

CENTRAL AND SOUTHERN COAST
6 CANAL CREEK
7 CAPE BLANCO STATE PARK
8 CAPE PERPETUA SCENIC AREA
9 EEL CREEK
10 ILLAHE
11 MARYS PEAK

NORTHERN CASCADES AND ENVIRONS
12 BADGER LAKE
13 BEAVERTAIL
14 CAMP CREEK
15 EAGLE CREEK
16 ELK LAKE
17 ELKHORN VALLEY
18 HOOVER
19 OXBOW REGIONAL PARK
20 SILVER FALLS STATE PARK
21 SUMMIT LAKE

CENTRAL CASCADES AND ENVIRONS
22 FRISSELL CROSSING
23 LOWER PALISADES

24 MALLARD MARSH
25 RIVERSIDE
26 THREE CREEK LAKE & DRIFTWOOD
27 TRAILBRIDGE
28 TUMALO STATE PARK
29 WILDCAT
30 YELLOWBOTTOM

SOUTHERN CASCADES AND ENVIRONS
31 FOURMILE LAKE
32 HEAD OF THE RIVER
33 LOST CREEK
34 NATURAL BRIDGE
35 RUJADA
36 SACANDAGA
37 THIELSEN VIEW
38 TIMPANOGAS

EASTERN OREGON
39 ANTHONY LAKES
40 BUCKHORN
41 DAIRY POINT
42 HIDDEN
43 JUBILEE LAKE
44 MINAM STATE RECREATION AREA
45 OLIVE LAKE
46 PAGE SPRINGS
47 SOUTH FORK
48 STRAWBERRY
49 TWO PAN
50 WALLOWA LAKE STATE PARK

ACKNOWLEDGMENTS

THIS BOOK CAME ABOUT with the assistance of numerous people who provided information, guidance, feedback, insights, and most importantly, encouragement. Specifically, I'd like to thank:

All of the National Forest Service, Bureau of Land Management, and individual park staff who provided accurate information, campground layouts, and other vital information to make these entries as exact as possible. They often had to dig deep and they came up with exactly what I needed when I needed it.

Rich and Val Allyn of Depoe Bay, Oregon, who were the delightful camp hosts at Tumalo State Park in Bend and who took time from their busy schedules to visit and write about the Canal Creek Campground when I was unable to get there myself.

Susan "Trooper" Cooper of Anacortes, Washington, for accompanying me on the first road trip, for enduring the hard lessons learned, and for the friendship that survived.

Gail Thomas of Atlanta, Georgia, for being a godsend of a summer housemate/catsitter, for tolerating my crazy schedule and Ozzie and Harriet's fickle, 18-year-old ways, and for bringing a new, unexpected friendship.

Harry Harpoon, currently of the San Francisco Bay area, whom I met in Joseph, Oregon, for his musical inspiration and kindred literary, camping, and nature-loving spirit.

PREFACE

TEN YEARS AGO, a modest little camping guide entitled *The Best in Tent Camping: Washington and Oregon* appeared on bookstore shelves and occasionally in window displays around the Pacific Northwest. It was my first published work of any substance, and I was both humbled by its juxtaposition next to works by legendary writers of the outdoor world and, truthfully, just a smidgen in awe of my own accomplishment. Perhaps because I had a background in publishing, I, more than most authors, knew what it took behind the scenes to bring one of these little miracles to fruition. I vowed I would never write another book again!

Well, three editions and at least three printings later, guess what? There's a sucker born every minute . . . In the spring of 2003, somewhere deep in the recesses of my practical mind, a diabolical demon rose up and refused to be ignored. His name was Bud Zehmer, and he was my editor.

Thanks to Bud, I had one of the most delightfully nerve-wracking summers of my life. I ventured back into the bush and, against all conceivable odds, surfaced with the campground quota to fill two separate editions. The result of the dogged and determined (often bordering on ludicrous) quest for the new Oregon book is presented here. Washington State will follow in Spring, 2005. (For the record, Bud is now pursuing a career in the ministry somewhere in an undisclosed location and Russell Helms, his successor, ought to be considering the same, as he has truly been a saint. Me? I'm heading for the nearest four-star hotel and a week-long room service binge!)

In all seriousness, the road research for this new edition put me to the ultimate test of physical endurance and mental perseverance. The summer and early fall of 2003 were fraught with horribly destructive forest fires in the West, record-setting temperatures, desperately low precipitation, and the highest gas prices since the embargo of the early 1970s! In addition, a realization was crystallizing slowly but steadily that finding quality tent camping in the Northwest today is a test, in varying proportions, of patience, timing, tolerance, and confidence. Patience with new regulatory systems and funding priorities. Timing to find the perfect spot before (or after) the crowds amass. Tolerance for the mindset (warning: gross generalization follows) that seems to go hand-in-hand with operating an RV or fifth-wheeler. Confidence to take that extra leap of faith into the unknown, which often leads down a bumpy dirt road.

Well, bad roads have a solution—drive slower—and confidence is gained through experience. Patience, as we're reminded from early childhood on, is a virtue. Timing is largely a matter of luck. As for tolerance, I'm still chewing on that one. Car camping in North America has taken a noticeable turn in favor of recreational vehicles in the decade since the first edition in the *Best in Tent Camping* series was published. Having been an avid backpacker, river rafter, cyclist, and general outdoor enthusiast all my life (30 years of which have been spent in the West), I find the trend towards accommodating RVs disturbing. The publication of this separate edition of *The Best in Tent Camping: Oregon* is therefore all the more important for preserving, both in print and practice, the fast-fading habit of enjoying the outdoors in a simple, uncomplicated, and relatively undisturbed manner.

The wilderness experience has become even more elusive than it was ten years ago. Public lands are seemingly dominated by the "V" factor–RV, SUV, ATV, Humvee. I wish I had kept count of the times I started up a road with a sign warning, "Not recommended for RVs or trailers" and, sure enough, there they'd be when I got to the campground. It became a bit of a game, but since I was the only one playing, I quickly got bored. Plus, it wasn't much of a contest. The "V" factor was winning practically every time!

Nevertheless, I'm happy to say that my car-camping research produced discoveries befitting the criteria that has shaped the books in this growing series from the start. I was also quite pleased to see that most of the Oregon entries from the original book have held up over time, and are included here with a little freshening up, alongside a host of new listings.

It's a demanding life trying to provide the discerning public with quality tent camping options, but I am honored to take on the task. I can't guarantee you'll camp in solitary splendor at the locations in this book, and I, sure as hell, won't be smug enough to proclaim them RV-free. But, hey, I tried. And I hope you will, too. For my own selfish interest and job security, I sincerely hope that the demand for serene and rustic camping will continue indefinitely, but it's up to us tent campers to make sure that it does. So, get out there, and don't let the RVs get you down.

Cheers and happy camping,
—Jeanne Louise Pyle

THE BEST IN TENT CAMPING

A GUIDE FOR CAR CAMPERS WHO HATE RVs,
CONCRETE SLABS, AND LOUD PORTABLE STEREOS

OREGON

FIRST EDITION

INTRODUCTION

FROM ROCKY COASTLINES TO ALPINE MEADOWS to sagebrush deserts, Oregon is a place of unparalleled beauty and diversity. Extremes of climate, terrain, and vegetation can be experienced in a single day's outing. The campgrounds included in this book are representative of the variety that makes Oregon such a prized destination for those who seek outstanding outdoor adventures.

And for those who value an experience that is long on solitude, serenity, and space, be aware that you may have to seek adventure farther afield than most. To escape the crowds, you must drive farther, climb higher, and plan more creatively. Although Oregon ranks third behind Alaska and Washington in designated wilderness acreage, it still constitutes only a little more than three percent of the state's total amount of land. More and more people flock beyond city limits to these scenic natural splendors, pushing the state's wilderness boundaries to capacity.

Encountering RVs in the most unlikely of places, as I did in my travels last year, one has to wonder if it isn't more comforting to think of wilderness as a state of mind rather than an actual place. I have observed that for some tent campers, it is satisfaction enough just to pitch a tent alongside several hundred others in midsummer at the busy, nearby state park. For others, simply being able to drive to the campground eliminates it from consideration. If your sentiment lies somewhere between these two extremes, you should find the offerings in this book appealing.

One trend I noticed in the course of my research comes as a bit of a "good news, bad news," but I prefer to view it as an encouraging sign. In the larger, more developed campgrounds run by the various agencies that have a hand in developing, managing, and maintaining the public lands of Oregon, it is now not uncommon to find a loop of sites designated as "tent camping" and another defined as "RV/Trailers." The tent camping sites are more rustic, without an electric hookup and usually with thicker vegetation between sites. The bad news is that they often get taken by the overflow of rigs and trailers, who squeeze themselves into the parking spaces. One problem solved; another created. Still, it's good to see that there is sensitivity to two very different styles of camping within the same compound.

Naturally, there are factors besides crowds that impact every camping trip, from a last minute trip to the outskirts of town to a backcountry outing planned months in advance. Here is some information that will prove useful, whether you are a first-time camper in Oregon or a veteran (you can always use a few reminders).

GEOGRAPHIC REGIONS

For a traveler, the most obvious distinction within Oregon is the difference in climate, terrain, and to some degree, lifestyle between the western and eastern regions of the state. The rugged coast and the Cascade mountains, which run north–south through the state, are generally considered Western Oregon, while Eastern Oregon, though larger geograph-ically, is sparsely populated and includes vast stretches of arid land. For ease in planning your trip, however, we have further grouped campgrounds into six regions, dividing those along the coast into northern and southern groups, dividing those in the Cascades (home to a prepoderance of Oregon's campgrounds) into northern, central, and southern groups, and presenting the scattered offerings of Eastern Oregon in a single group. If you intend, for example, to make Crater Lake the primary destination for your camping trip, you will first want to review campgrounds in the Southern Cascades. The map and key on pages viii and ix provide an overview of the campgrounds profiled in this guide and their respective geographic regions.

WEATHER

Prevailing conditions year-round (with a few exceptions) in western Oregon are mild and damp. Not so much rain, as a healthy supply of gray clouds and mist. Areas like the Willamette Valley on the eastern flanks of the Coast Range can get quite hot and steamy, but a short drive up and over the range to the coastal areas and you'll be reaching for the fleece as the inversion effect creates fog banks and cool breezes. Late summer and early fall are the most dependable seasons for lovely stints of dry, sunny, warm days just about anywhere in western Oregon.

In eastern Oregon, conditions are desert-like, with hot and dry summers. Severe thunderstorms can be the biggest threat to outdoor activity and, in turn, can spark instan-taneous wildfires and flash floods. At higher elevations on both western and eastern mountain slopes, snow is not uncommon, even in midsummer. Sudden changes in weather conditions are always a consideration, so pack accordingly.

ROAD CONDITIONS AND DIRECTIONS

Many of the campgrounds in this book are reached by minimally maintained access roads. Since we were looking for spots that are somewhat off the beaten path (and away from the most-traveled routes for those dreaded RVs), access roads can be rougher than you might expect. Inquire about current road conditions before venturing too far if you are unsure of what you may encounter and be sure that you have a current road atlas with you.

The maps in this book are designed to help orient you, nothing more. Although we've provided directions at the end of each entry, you'll still need detailed maps to get in and out of most of the campgrounds. The local and district offices that oversee most of these campgrounds are the best source for detailed maps (see Appendix B for more infor-mation on these agencies).

Standardized road designations appear throughout the text in accordance with the following examples: I-5 for Interstate 5, US 101 for U.S. Highway 101, OR 58 for Oregon Highway 58, SR 205 for State Road 205, CR 40 for County Road 40, and FS 15 for Forest Service Road 15.

RESTRICTIONS

Increased visitation to natural areas usually means more restrictions. State and federal agencies manage most of the campgrounds in this book. Check with the proper authorities for current regulations on recreational activities, such as permits for day-use parking, backcountry travel, hunting and fishing, mountain bikes in designated areas, etc. We have included some restrictions in the Key Information sections of each campground description, but because restrictions can change, you still need to check before you go. Be aware that many national forest and State Park parking areas now require day-use fees or annual passes. Passes can be purchased at any forest service office or ranger station, and at numerous campgrounds and oudoor retailer outlets.

FIRES

Campfire regulations are subject to seasonal conditions. Usually there are signs posted at campgrounds or ranger district offices. Please be sure you are aware of the current situation and NEVER make a campfire anywhere other than in existing fire pits at developed sites. Never, ever toss a match or cigarette idly in the brush or alongside the road. It's not only littering, it can also trigger the incineration of that beautiful forest you were just admiring.

WATER

Many of the campgrounds in this book are remote enough that piped water is not available. No matter how remote you may think you are, though, don't risk drinking straight from mountain streams, creeks, and lakes. Oregon has some of the purest natural waters in the world, but it is not immune to that nasty parasite called *Giardia lamblia,* which causes horrific stomach cramps and long-term diarrhea. If you don't have drinking water or purification tablets with you, boil any untreated water for at least five minutes. This will seem like a hassle if you're dry as a bone at the end of a long day of activity, but believe me, the agony you will avoid makes it worth the wait.

THE RATING SYSTEM

Within the scope of the campground criteria for this book—accessible by car, scenic, and as close to a wilderness setting as possible—each campground offers its own characteristics. The best way to deal with these varying attributes was to devise a rating system that highlights each campground's best features. On our five-star ranking system, five is the highest rating and one is the lowest. So if you're looking for a campground that is scenic and achingly quiet, look for five stars in the Beauty and Quiet categories. If you're more interested in a campground that has excellent security and cavernous campsites, look for five stars in the

Spaciousness and Security categories. Keep in mind that these ratings are based somewhat on the subjective views of the author and her sources.

BEAUTY

If this category needs explanation at all, it is simply to say that the true beauty of a campground is not always what you can see but what you can't see. Or hear. Like a freeway. Or roaring motorboats. Or the crack, pop, pop, boom of a rifle range. An equally important factor for me is the condition of the campground itself—and to what extent it has been left in its natural state. Beauty, of course, also takes into consideration any fabulous views of mountains, waterfalls, or other natural phenomena.

SITE PRIVACY

No one who enjoys the simplicity of tent camping wants to be walled in on all sides by RVs the size of tractor trailers. This category goes hand in hand with the previous one, because in part a campsite's beauty relies on the privacy of its surroundings. If you've ever crawled out of your tent to embrace a stunning summer morning in your skivvies and found several pairs of curious eyes staring at you from the neighbor's picture window, you know what I mean. I look for campsites that are graciously spaced with lots of heavy foliage in between. You can often find more private sites by driving a little deeper into the campground complex.

SPACIOUSNESS

I'm not as much of a stickler for size because I'm happy if there's room to park the car off the main campground road, enough space to pitch a two- or four-man tent in a reasonably flat and dry spot, a picnic table, and a fire pit safely away from the tenting area. At most campgrounds, site spaciousness is sacrificed for site privacy and vice versa. Sometimes you get extremely lucky and have both. Don't be greedy.

QUIET

Again, this category coincides with the beauty field. When I go camping, I want to hear the sounds of nature. You know, birds chirping, the wind sighing, a surf crashing, a brook babbling. Call me crazy . . . it's not always possible to control the noise volume of your fellow campers, so the closer you can get to natural sounds that can drown them out, the better. Actually, when you have a chance to listen to the quiet of nature, you'll find that it is really rather noisy. But what a lovely cacophony!

SECURITY

Quite a few of the campgrounds in this book are in remote and primitive places without on-site security patrols. In essence, you're on your own. Common sense is a great asset in these cases. Don't leave expensive outdoor gear or valuable camera equipment lying around your campsite—or even within view inside your car. If you are at a hosted site, you may feel more comfortable leaving any valuables with the host (if they're willing). Or let them know when you'll be gone for an extended period so they can keep an eye on your things. Unfortunately, even in lightly camped areas, vandalism is a common camping problem. In many places, wild animals can do as much damage as a human being. If you leave food inside your tent or around the campsite, don't be surprised if things look slightly ransacked when you return. The most frequent visitors to food-strewn campsites are birds, squirrels, chipmunks, deer, and bears.

CLEANLINESS

By and large, all the campgrounds in this book rank highly in this category. I think Oregon campgrounds are some of the cleanest and tidiest I've stayed in due to the fine management of park and Forest Service attendants. The only time they tend to fall a bit short of expectation is on busy summer weekends. This is usually only the case for larger, more developed compounds. In more remote areas, the level of cleanliness is most often dependent on the good habits of campers themselves. Keep that in mind wherever you camp. If the sign says, "Pack it in, pack it out," do as you're told. You can dump your garbage at the first gas station. DON'T expect someone to pick up after you at the campsite.

INSECT CONTROL

Spraying for bugs is not a regular practice in Oregon campgrounds. If the campground is situated on a lake (particularly at higher elevations), you can almost bet that mosquitoes will be a nuisance in midsummer. Even if the campground has earned a high insect control rating, it's always a good idea to have a reliable repellent in your cache of camping essentials. Everyone reacts to (and is affected by) the presence of bugs differently. The most common winged critters that cause problems are mosquitoes, no-see-ums, deer flies, sand fleas, and ticks.

CHANGES

While campgrounds are less prone to change than big-time tourist attractions, they are nevertheless subject to agency budgets, upgrades and dilapidation, and even natural disasters. With that in mind, it's a good idea to call ahead for the most updated report on the campground you've selected. We appreciate being told about any notable changes that you come across while using this book and welcome all reader input, including suggestions for potential entries for future editions. Send them to the author care of Menasha Ridge Press at the address provided on page iv.

NORTHERN COAST

BEVERLY BEACH STATE PARK CAMPGROUND

WHILE YOU MAY THINK of the Pacific Coast as a summer destination, Oregon steps to the beat of a different drummer. Many people flock to the rugged Oregon coast to watch the winter storms and look out for whales. In fact, the prime whale-watching months are from late December to mid-March, when volunteers set up camp specifically to help you spot the spouts at prime locations along the coast.

Located seven miles north of Newport, Beverly Beach is a must-stay campground if you're in the area. While many of the surrounding campgrounds can get overloaded with RVs and consequently feel a little cramped, this campground manages to host everyone and still make you feel like you've gotten away from it all (and from your neighbor). The sites are spacious and wooded, and a nature trail winds its way through the campground, so you can get a little exercise to start off your day.

The most scenic part of the nature trail follows Spencer Creek, which borders the campground to the south. Access the trail near site C-7. After crossing Spencer Creek, the trail splits. Walking to the right takes you to the hiker/biker camp. Head left to walk along the creek. The trail follows the creek to a bridge crossing located near site G-16. If you like to bicycle, park roads are open to bikes (helmets required).

Divided into eight loops, the campground is large, with 128 tent sites—trailers of any kind are wisely forbidden in the tent-camping areas. There are also five group tent-camping areas.

One attraction of this campground is that you can walk to the beach from your tent site through a tunnel under the highway, allowing for front-row seats to watch the sun set. While there are some sites

> *You'll get all the creature comforts here, but you can also lose yourself in the spacious sites at this beachside campground.*

RATINGS

Beauty: ✩ ✩ ✩ ✩
Privacy: ✩ ✩ ✩
Spaciousness: ✩ ✩ ✩ ✩
Quiet: ✩ ✩
Security: ✩ ✩ ✩
Cleanliness: ✩ ✩ ✩
Insect Control: ✩ ✩ ✩

ADDRESS: Beverly Beach State
Park
198 NW 123rd Street
Newport, OR 97365

OPERATED BY: Oregon State Parks

INFORMATION: (541) 265-9278,
(800) 452-5687;
www.oregonstate
parks.org

OPEN: Year-round

SITES: 128

EACH SITE HAS: Picnic table, fire ring

ASSIGNMENT: First come, first
served or by reser-
vation at (800) 452-
5687 or www.reserve
america.com ($6 fee)

REGISTRATION: At the campground
entrance

FACILITIES: Flush toilets, hot
showers

PARKING: At campsites only

FEE: $13 per night
(October–April); $16
(May–September)

ELEVATION: Sea level

RESTRICTIONS: **Pets:** On leash only
Fires: At fire rings
only
Alcohol: Permitted
Vehicles: One per
site; $7 per addi-
tional vehicle
Other: 14-day stay
limit

closer to the beach, they tend to get bombarded with visitors, so don't be fooled into thinking those are the best spots. Generally, the farther you are from the beach, the more likely you are to have some solitude. If you like to surf, the north beach is recommended. If you want to look for fossils, walk south along the beach.

With a general store nearby, firewood available at the campground, a campground entrance station where staff will fill you in on the recreation hot spots, not to mention flush toilets and hot showers, Beverly Beach is a prime spot for tent-camping luxury with some elbow room.

Hiking is a popular activity here, with plenty of lighthouses (in particular, Yaquina Head lighthouse is just south of the campground) and viewpoints to explore right off famous US 101. Of course, simply driving is a sight-seeing exploration in itself, as the sweeping cliffside views of waves crashing below will tempt you to get out of your car and take advantage of the viewpoints. Just north of Cape Foulweather, visit Depoe Bay and its remarkable spouting horn. When ocean waves surge into rocky tunnels along the shore, the spout erupts á la Old Faithful.

In addition, Newport is 7 miles south, so you can get a fix of coastal city charm at the historic water-front (and sample some famous Moe's Clam Chowder). Established in 1882, Newport is a small town along the Yaquina bay waterfront. Newport also has charter rentals, if you want to get out on the water, and the Oregon Coast Aquarium is just a few miles away. In fact, there's so much to do in the surround-ing area, it's a good thing Beverly Beach is open year-round, so you can pick your pleasure.

MAP

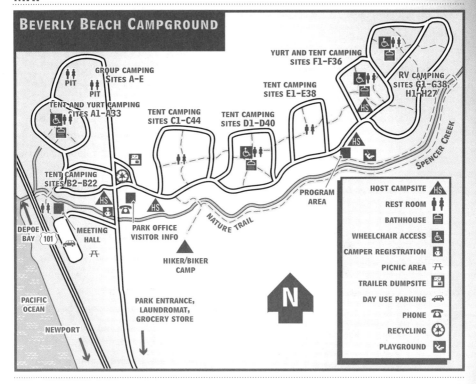

BEVERLY BEACH CAMPGROUND

GROUP CAMPING SITES A-E

PIT
PIT

TENT AND YURT CAMPING SITES A1-A33

YURT AND TENT CAMPING SITES F1-F36

TENT CAMPING SITES E1-E38

RV CAMPING SITES G1-G38, H1-H27

HS

TENT CAMPING SITES C1-C44

TENT CAMPING SITES D1-D40

HS

SPENCER CREEK

TENT CAMPING SITES B2-B22

HS

HS

PROGRAM AREA

NATURE TRAIL

DEPOE BAY 101

MEETING HALL

PARK OFFICE VISITOR INFO

HIKER/BIKER CAMP

N

PACIFIC OCEAN

NEWPORT

PARK ENTRANCE, LAUNDROMAT, GROCERY STORE

HOST CAMPSITE	HS
REST ROOM	
BATHHOUSE	
WHEELCHAIR ACCESS	
CAMPER REGISTRATION	
PICNIC AREA	
TRAILER DUMPSITE	
DAY USE PARKING	
PHONE	
RECYCLING	
PLAYGROUND	

GETTING THERE

From Newport, drive 7 miles north on US 101 to the park entrance on the right (east) side of the highway.

CAPE LOOKOUT STATE PARK CAMPGROUND

> *Superb views, wildlife refuges, and historic sites make Cape Lookout a popular destination for weekenders and summer vacationers from Oregon's metropolitan areas.*

RATINGS

Beauty: ☆ ☆ ☆ ☆ ☆
Privacy: ☆ ☆ ☆ ☆
Spaciousness: ☆ ☆ ☆
Quiet: ☆ ☆ ☆ (summer)
      ☆ ☆ ☆ ☆ (winter)
Security: ☆ ☆ ☆ ☆
Cleanliness: ☆ ☆ ☆ ☆ ☆
Insect Control: ☆ ☆ ☆

THE FIRST OF THREE campgrounds in what I like to refer to as the "cape-camping collection" is the lovely and linear Cape Lookout State Park, just south of Netarts on the Three Capes Scenic Drive (for the other two campgrounds, see pages 27 and 30). The route actually encompasses two more state parks with (as you may have guessed from the road's name) magnificent headlands—Cape Meares on the north and Cape Kiwanda on the south—but these are day-use facilities only.

As a team, Cape Lookout, Cape Meares, and Cape Kiwanda are a formidable panoply of public lands and the centerpiece of more than 2,500 acres of coastal rain forest, sheer cliffs, wide sandy beaches and dunes, narrow spits, rocky points and outcroppings, protected bays, and estuaries.

To accommodate the sizable numbers of seashore enthusiasts, the well-maintained and efficiently designed Cape Lookout State Park offers a whopping 176 tent sites, many of which are accessible all year. In addition, it offers a separate hiker-and-biker camp not far from the central camping grounds. Group camps are also available, as well as a meeting hall and four cabins. Despite the number of campsites, there is a spaciousness and openness about the place so that it feels—dare I say it?—uncrowded. That's not likely to be the case on any given summer day, but enjoy the feeling when you can. It's due in large part to the fact that when you have your back to the cape, the view is mainly of sand dunes, saltwater, and sky, a heady combination that encourages mindless meandering and musing. But if you insist on a mission, consider shell collecting, birdwatching, whalespotting (at the right times of year), and the like.

Geologically speaking, it may come as a surprise that the exquisite cape formations in this area and all along the Oregon Coast are the wind-, weather-, and wave-carved remains of ancient volcanoes. Geologists speculate that massive Cape Lookout, considered by many to be one of the most scenic capes in the Northwest, originally formed as an island off the coast when a huge lava flow cooled and congealed differently above and below sea level. You can observe the geologic layers from the base of this 700-foot promontory. The Cape Meares formation occurred similarly.

Cape Kiwanda, however, is essentially compressed sand made rock and then shoved upward. Its sandstone composition would normally make Cape Kiwanda a fragile target of the pounding surf, but as if by a master plan, nature provided the lofty point with its own Haystack Rock. (The more famous one is farther north, off the coast of Cannon Beach.) This giant piece of basalt encumbers incoming waves so effectively that fishing boats can head directly into the subdued breakers. In honor of this phenomenon, Pacific City (south of Cape Kiwanda) holds the Pacific City Dory Derby each summer, showing off the seafaring talents of its famous fleet of flat-bottomed boats.

The Cape Meares cliffs are the nesting grounds for a wide variety of shorebirds that are protected, along with their forest-dwelling counterparts, by Cape Meares National Wildlife Refuge and Three Arch Rock National Wildlife Refuge in Oceanside. Between the two refuges, more than 150 species of birds are known to inhabit the shores and uplands. Cape Meares is also the site of the "Octopus Tree," a Sitka spruce gone wild, with an inordinate number of drooping branches. Historic Tillamook Light lighthouse on Cape Meares is the structural centerpiece of this park. As of this writing, the 113-year-old lighthouse was closed for renovation but is scheduled to reopen in 2004.

The average 90 inches of annual rainfall keep things fairly wet in winter and struggling to dry out in summer. If you dress appropriately, hiking the headlands and watching storms roll in can be an exhilarating winter adventure along this stretch of Oregon coast. The Cape Lookout Trail alone traces the headland for more than 2 miles, with a total of 8 miles of trails through old-growth forest. Several trails offer

KEY INFORMATION

ADDRESS:	Cape Lookout State Park 13000 Whiskey Creek Road West Tillamook, OR 97141
OPERATED BY:	Oregon State Parks
INFORMATION:	(503) 842-4981, (800) 551-6949; www.oregonstate parks.org
OPEN:	Year-round
SITES:	176 tent; 38 full-hookup, 1 electric; separate group site and hiker/biker camp
EACH SITE HAS:	Picnic table, fire pit and grill, piped water, shade trees
ASSIGNMENT:	First come, first served or by reservation at (800) 452-5687 or www.reserve america.com ($6 fee)
REGISTRATION:	On site
FACILITIES:	Flush toilets, hot water, showers; public telephone; day-use area ($3 per vehicle) has picnic tables, grills, and beach access; limited disabled access
PARKING:	At campsites
FEE:	Tents $17, $13 winter; full hookups $20, $16 winter; deluxe cabins $65, $45 winter; yurts $27; hiker/biker sites $4 per person; $7 per additional vehicle
ELEVATION:	Sea level
RESTRICTIONS:	**Pets:** On leash only **Fires:** In fire pits only **Alcohol:** Permitted **Vehicles:** No RV size limit **Other:** 14-day stay limit

MAP

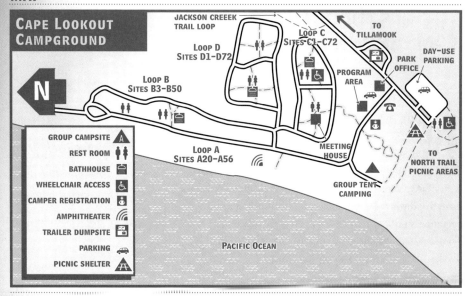

CAPE LOOKOUT CAMPGROUND

JACKSON CREEEK TRAIL LOOP

LOOP C SITES C1–C72

TO TILLAMOOK

LOOP D SITES D1–D72

DAY–USE PARK PARKING

PARK OFFICE

PROGRAM AREA

LOOP B SITES B3–B50

N

GROUP CAMPSITE A

REST ROOM

BATHHOUSE

WHEELCHAIR ACCESS

CAMPER REGISTRATION

AMPHITHEATER

TRAILER DUMPSITE

PARKING

PICNIC SHELTER A

LOOP A SITES A20–A56

MEETING HOUSE

TO NORTH TRAIL PICNIC AREAS

GROUP TENT CAMPING

PACIFIC OCEAN

GETTING THERE

To reach Cape Lookout from Tillamook, drive southwest on Netarts Highway, following signs for Cape Lookout State Park the entire way. The total distance from Tillamook is about 10 miles without any detours or side trips.

interpretive signage noting indigenous foliage and salmon restoration efforts. Keep in mind that many of these trails are steep and slick in places. Safer and equally as interesting is the 5-mile stroll along Cape Lookout State Park's sand spit, between the ocean and Netarts Bay.

In the bay's calm waters, you'll find conditions ideal for crabbing, either by boat or from the shore. Supplies can be found in town, and several places will cook your catch for you. Clamming and fishing are other options.

If you run out of things to do (which is unlikely) and want to play tourist, Tillamook is nearby. It has a history museum and tours of its renowned cheese factory. If you're wondering about those huge aluminum barns you can see from US 101 out in the middle of a pasture, I've been told that they house old dirigibles, relics of a bygone age of aviation. I'm waiting for the day they open these to the public.

DOVRE, ELK BEND, AND THE NESTUCCA RIVER CAMPGROUNDS

Blaine

NOT TOO FAR BUT definitely out there, the Bureau of Land Mangement campgrounds on the Nestucca River are easily accessible via the official Nestucca Scenic Byway scenic a short drive west of tMcMinnville in the Willamette Valley. You have the distinct feeling that you've stumbled upon someone's private party when you arrive there. They're that intimate—and largely unknown to the hordes that congregate along the coast.

Five BLM facilities comprise the Nestucca River chain of campgrounds; from east to west, they are Dovre, Fan Creek, Elk Bend, Alder Glen, and Rocky Bend. Collectively, they offer an extraordinary selection of 43 tent-camping sites spread across 12 miles of beautiful forested river frontage, so I decided to lump them all together. Take your pick or try them all.

The campgrounds are under the jurisdiction of the BLM's Salem District office (although Rocky Bend is officially a Siuslaw Forest Service campground that is managed jointly with the BLM). The sites are also part of the Tillamook Resource Area, a massive designation that encompasses facilities all the way from the Yaquina Lighthouse on the coast to the Quartzville Recreation Corridor south and east near Sweet Home. True to BLM management style, the sites along the Nestucca are well-designed (albeit compact), primitive sites tucked along the banks of the river. They range in altitude from 700 feet at Rocky Bend up to 1,500 feet at Dovre.

Of the five, as far as tent camping goes, Elk Bend has the most going for it. It is walk-in only with five sites and there is no fee. Rocky Bend has six sites and is also no fee, but it is not walk-in; the three other campgrounds have either 10 or 11 campsites and the fee is $6 per night and $4 for each additional vehicle. Elk Bend

> *Take your pick from this collection of BLM campgrounds that offer solitude, scenery and riverside settings.*

RATINGS

Beauty: ✪ ✪ ✪ ✪ ✪
Privacy: ✪ ✪ ✪
Spaciousness: ✪ ✪ ✪
Quiet: ✪ ✪ ✪ ✪
Security: ✪ ✪
Cleanliness: ✪ ✪ ✪ ✪ ✪
Insect Control: ✪ ✪

ADDRESS: Tillamook Resource
Area
Bureau of Land
Management,
Salem District
1717 Fabry Road SE
Salem, OR 97306

OPERATED BY: Bureau of Land
Management

INFORMATION: (503) 375-5646

OPEN: April through
November

SITES: 43 total

EACH SITE HAS: Picnic table, fire grill

ASSIGNMENT: First come, first
served; no reserva-
tions

REGISTRATION: Self-registration on
site

FACILITIES: Vault toilets, hand-
pumped water,
group shelter with
fire grill

PARKING: At campsites

FEE: $6, $4 per additional
vehicle

ELEVATION: 700–1,500 feet

RESTRICTIONS: **Pets:** On leash only
Fires: In fire pits
only
Alcohol: Permitted
Vehicles: RVs up to
21 feet; no hookups
Other: 14-day stay
limit; only some sites
are wheelchair
accessible

and Rocky Bend stay open all year long; the others operate between early April and the end of November.

All campgrounds have piped water except Rocky Bend. All but Elk Bend offer wheelchair accessibility at some sites. Picnic tables and fire pits are standard issue in each campsite. Dovre has one group shelter with its own fire pit. Alder Glen sports its own fishing pier. All garbage must be packed out of all sites.

Unless you're an avid angler, don't even think about vying for a spot along the Nestucca during the height of fall steelhead and spring and summer chinook runs. The river is known throughout the western hemisphere for its excellent runs of both species, as well as a year-round stocked supply of cutthroat trout.

If you are a paddler, be mindful that running the river at its peak (most likely when the fish are running as well) carries the risk of getting tangled in fishing lines. Hopefully, there's room for everyone. The rains in winter can produce a good volume of water for boaters, but the river can also achieve flood stage quickly. Use common sense, and certainly don't boat alone in peak-flow periods.

The main attraction of the Nestucca Scenic Byway is the river itself and activities that relate to it. However, the coast and all its fascinations are not far away. Driving through the lowland meadows and farmlands on your way there, you may get sidetracked by the quaint villages that stay alive thanks to busy US 101 but retain a few artifacts from their pre-tourism heritage. Don't blink or you'll miss Blaine, where the Nestucca Byway takes a hard left to the west. Then comes Beaver at the byway's junction with US 101. Heading south, Hebo is home to the district office of the Siuslaw National Forest, a good place for maps and information. Cloverdale calls itself "Oregon's Best Kept Secret," and I guess most people who breeze through would agree.

Hiking options are not immediately apparent at the Nestucca campgrounds. The forest lands surrounding the Nestucca River are broken up into a mix of federal, state, and private stewardship. It's difficult to know whose territory you might be invading, so it is a

MAP

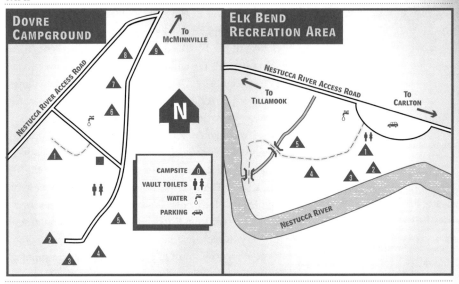

DOVRE CAMPGROUND

To McMinnville

8 9 7 6 1 5 2 3 4

N

CAMPSITE	0
VAULT TOILETS	
WATER	
PARKING	

ELK BEND RECREATION AREA

NESTUCCA RIVER ACCESS ROAD

To TILLAMOOK

To CARLTON

5 4 3 2 1

NESTUCCA RIVER

good idea to check with either the Siuslaw National Forest, BLM, or Tillamook State Forest authorities. Recognizable hiking trails are not too far away on Mount Hebo, where you can walk through some very old second-growth forest or clamber along an even older pioneer road converted to trail. Although there's a trail to the summit of Mount Hebo for die-hard hikers, you can also drive up for expansive views of the Nestucca Valley and west to the Pacific.

GETTING THERE

From SR 47 in Carlton (north of McMinnville), turn west on Meadow Lake Road, which becomes Nestucca River Access Road (also known as the Nestucca Scenic Byway). Follow this for 17 miles to the campground. There are numerous side roads that depart from the main road, so check road signs occasionally to make sure you're on the right track. From the coast, the Nestucca River Road is accessed off US 101 in Beaver on Blaine Road just north of Hebo. Once again, follow signs as the road takes many jogs and twists.

OSWALD WEST STATE PARK CAMPGROUND

> *One of Oregon's best state park campgrounds, Oswald offers primitive walk-in sites in an inner sanctum of coastal rain forest.*

OF THE MANY GEMS IN OREGON'S extensive state park system, which helps make camping in the state such a pleasurable experience, Oswald West is a crown jewel.

It is a rather unique gem, actually. There are 30 primitive walk-in tent sites reached by a 0.3-mile trail from the parking area. The state park provides wheelbarrows for carting your camp gear up and down the angled, paved pathway. Part of the camaraderie that quickly develops on a camping trip to Oswald comes from exchanging greetings, sympathy, and an occasional helping hand with fellow campers offer as they push, pull, tug, and otherwise maneuver their overloaded carts between car and campsite. It is not unusual to find a heap of spilled goods lying in the path as a frustrated youngster valiantly attempts to right his overturned one-wheeled craft before Dad comes looking to see what in the world is taking so long.

It's all in the spirit of camping at Oswald West, but you can tell the veterans from the novices around here. They've learned to travel light.

The lush surroundings are probably the first thing you'll notice when you descend into this primeval coastal rain forest. The trees here look as old as time, soaring skyward and standing sentry in their heavy, shaggy coats of moss. The campsites are private little grottoes of greenery interspersed among the venerable collection of western red cedar, hemlock, and Sitka spruce. The entire campground is shrouded in a rich ground cover of salal, sword ferns, huckleberry, and salmonberry, with wildflowers such as trillium and skunk cabbage adding spots of color when in bloom.

Getting around the campground is easiest (not to mention highly recommended) by way of the established trails. It's easy to find yourself in someone else's

RATINGS

Beauty: ✪ ✪ ✪ ✪ ✪
Privacy: ✪ ✪ ✪ ✪
Spaciousness: ✪ ✪ ✪ ✪
Quiet: ✪ ✪ ✪ ✪
Security: ✪ ✪ ✪
Cleanliness: ✪ ✪ ✪ ✪
Insect Control: ✪

campsite if you're not paying attention, so respect others who are here for the same reasons as you—privacy and quietude. Crashing through the underbrush in a shortcut to the restroom is a definite camping faux pas. But to have flush toilets in an otherwise undeveloped facility is a rare treat indeed.

The Coast Range hugs the Pacific along this section of the Oregon coast, resulting in steep bluffs that rise dramatically above the shoreline but minimize the beaches below. Short Sands Beach (named in keeping with the geographic limitations) is tucked into the protective curve of Smuggler's Cove and is the only beachcombing option in an expanse of 2,500 acres of parkland that stretches from Arch Cape to Neahkahnie Beach. It's also a good spot to watch surfers and boogie boarders who have discovered the thrills and spills that come with threading through the rock "stacks" that dot these tricky waters. In higher tides, the surf can be quite intimidating as it swirls and crashes and spews. To me, it seems far too easy to get impaled on one of the rocks, especially when the powerful surging and sucking of the tide make the sea a frothing wash cycle, but everyone has their own form of foolhardy fun. I'll stick to tamer activities.

Like headlands hiking, for example. Both Cape Falcon and Neahkahnie Mountain have trails to the top for dramatic views. The 3-mile route up Neahkahnie zigzags its way to a 1,710-foot promontory, with views north that extend beyond the Columbia River. In all, there are 15 miles of trails in "Os West," as it is affectionately known by the locals. A dozen of these are part of the lengthy Oregon Coast Trail. Ask the park rangers for more information about this popular and unique trail.

Rain-forest conditions mean routine wet weather as the moisture-heavy marine clouds meet the unyielding Coast Range and dump their load on Oswald West. It can also be quite blustery. An extreme example came in 1982 when gales raging at more than 150 miles per hour leveled 6 million board feet of old-growth Sitka spruce on Cape Falcon. It took two years to replant the area, and it will take centuries of growth to compensate for the loss of those huge, old conifers.

KEY INFORMATION

ADDRESS:	Oswald West State Park 9500 Sandpiper Lane Nehalem, OR 97131
OPERATED BY:	Oregon State Parks
INFORMATION:	(503) 368-5943
OPEN:	March through October
SITES:	30 primitive, walk-in
EACH SITE HAS:	Picnic table, fire pit, piped water, shade trees
ASSIGNMENT:	First come, first served; no reservations
REGISTRATION:	Self-registration on site
FACILITIES:	Bathhouse with toilets, sinks, running water; wheelbarrows for transporting gear; firewood
PARKING:	In campground parking lot at trailhead
FEE:	$14, $10 October through April (a.k.a. Discovery Season); $7 per extra vehicle
ELEVATION:	Sea level
RESTRICTIONS:	Pets: On leash only Fires: In fire pits only Alcohol: Permitted Vehicles: No RV or trailer accommodations; no bicycles on park trails Other: 14-day stay limit

MAP

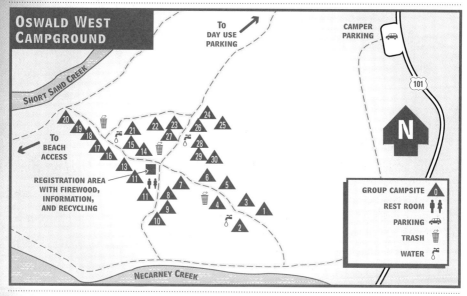

OSWALD WEST CAMPGROUND

To DAY USE PARKING

CAMPER PARKING

SHORT SAND CREEK

To BEACH ACCESS

REGISTRATION AREA WITH FIREWOOD, INFORMATION, AND RECYCLING

NECARNEY CREEK

GROUP CAMPSITE
REST ROOM
PARKING
TRASH
WATER

GETTING THERE

To arrive from Cannon Beach, drive south on US 101 for about 10 miles. Access to the campground is available from the southern-most parking lot, which may be full. Overflow parking areas are located nearby.

The park's peak season is June through August, but some of the best (i.e. dry and fog-free) weather occurs in September and October. In spring, Neahkahnie Mountain provides a splendid display of wildflowers in bloom, particularly the pink coast fawn lily.

SADDLE MOUNTAIN STATE PARK CAMPGROUND

WANT TO ENJOY THE BEACH, see the mountains, and not get trampled by the crowds? Saddle Mountain is the answer.

Most people hurrying along US 26 between Portland and the ocean beaches in northwestern Oregon pass up this cool, green spot, either because they don't know about it or they have an unusual idea of "getting away from it all" in the overdeveloped, overpriced, and overrun resorts, motels, inns, rental cottages, and RV parks in seaside towns from the mouth of the Columbia River to the California border.

Don't get me wrong. I love the Oregon coast. If you want to pay the price, there are scads of wonderful places to stay—for a day, weekend, or week. And there are still plenty of areas that have been preserved in an undeveloped state to showcase the natural coastal beauty. But if your interest is tent camping in the purest sense, the Oregon coast may be a disappointment. You'll have to sacrifice ocean proximity for optimum peace and quiet by going farther inland to places such as Saddle Mountain State Park.

However, you have the best of both worlds at Saddle Mountain, because you'll be less than 15 miles from the nearest coastal attractions of Cannon Beach and Seaside, well away from the crowded US 101 corridor and only a 2.6-mile hike from superb views from atop the park's namesake, the highest peak in northwestern Oregon. Not a bad combination, really.

Add to that a campground (albeit primitive) for tent campers only and nearly 3,000 acres (roughly 5 square miles) of second-growth forests, fragile meadows, and clear-running creeks. You'll share the terrain with a number of woodland critters (elk have been spotted in sizeable herds within the park) and a host of indigenous plantlife (more than 300 species have been identified), some that for reasons not altogether clear

> *If the summer crowds on the Oregon coast are more than you can handle but you don't want to forego scenic pleasures, consider Saddle Mountain State Park.*

RATINGS

Beauty: ✿ ✿
Privacy: ✿ ✿ ✿
Spaciousness: ✿ ✿
Quiet: ✿ ✿
Security: ✿ ✿
Cleanliness: ✿ ✿ ✿ ✿
Insect Control: ✿ ✿ ✿ ✿

ADDRESS: Saddle Mountain
State Park
P.O. Box 681
Cannon Beach, OR
97110

OPERATED BY: Oregon State Parks

INFORMATION: (503) 368-5943

OPEN: April through
November

SITES: 10

EACH SITE HAS: Picnic table, fire pit,
piped water, shade
trees

ASSIGNMENT: First come, first
served; no reserva-
tions

REGISTRATION: Self-registration on
site

FACILITIES: Rest rooms with toilets, sinks, running
water; firewood

PARKING: In campground

FEE: $9, $7 per additional
vehicle

ELEVATION: 1,650 feet

RESTRICTIONS: **Pets:** On leash only
Fires: In fire pits
only
Alcohol: Permitted
Vehicles: No RV or
trailer accommoda-
tions; self-contained
units may use park-
ing lot
Other: 14-day stay
limit

have chosen Saddle Mountain as their preferred habitat, growing only here and nowhere else in the Coast Range.

This latter feature will be of particular interest to the weekend botanist. Saddle Mountain was a haven for certain species of plant life during the Ice Age, and much of that flora evolved in ways peculiar to the Coast Range. Today, high on the flanks of this 3,283-foot peak, grow plants not found anywhere else. Patterson's bittercress is the most unique, found only on Saddle Mountain and nearby Onion Mountain. The best time to visit Saddle Mountain is early to mid-June, when the alpine wildflowers put on one of the most colorful shows in the region.

For the weekend mountaineer, Saddle Mountain Trail is a pleasantly surprising challenge, with a reward of unending views from the summit. Casual hikers will probably want to stop at the saddle just beyond the wildflower fields. The more adventurous and sure-footed in your party can continue on to the crest, but be forewarned that the path is steep and indistinct in places, making travel, as the park brochure says, "extremely treacherous" and not recommended for those who aren't in the best of shape.

Those who do make it to the top can feast on the views while enjoying a picnic lunch. To the south are Nehalem Bay and a sprinkle of small, characteristic coastal towns. Looking west, the Pacific Ocean paints a blue-green backdrop to the resort towns of Seaside and Cannon Beach, with Tillamook Head and Haystack Rock figuring prominently between them. Northward is historic Astoria where the Columbia River meets the Pacific. Fort Clatsop is the site of Lewis and Clark's winter camp in 1805 and 1806. Snowcapped Cascade Mountain peaks to the east add a finishing touch.

The weather is not always conducive to uninterrupted vistas on the slopes of Saddle Mountain and can easily change for the worse between the time you leave your campsite and make the roundtrip hike of less than 7 miles. With an elevation differential of more than 2,000 feet, the temperature is often much warmer at the campground than at the summit, too, so keep that in mind as you pack your sack. Ocean breezes can also

MAP

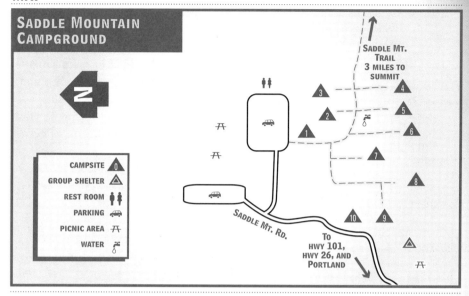

SADDLE MOUNTAIN CAMPGROUND

SADDLE MT. TRAIL 3 MILES TO SUMMIT

CAMPSITE	0
GROUP SHELTER	⚠
REST ROOM	♂ ♀
PARKING	🚐
PICNIC AREA	🪵
WATER	🚰

SADDLE MT. RD.

To HWY 101, HWY 26, AND PORTLAND

have a chilling effect, even if the sun is bright. And in the most fierce conditions, the maritime Pacific climate has been known to dump upwards of 100 inches of rain annually, so be prepared for wet conditions anytime.

GETTING THERE

To reach Saddle Mountain State Park, turn north on Saddle Mountain Road off US 26 about 1.5 miles east of Necanicum Junction. Drive 7 miles to the campground. A picnic area, parking lot (self-contained RVs can park here), and trailhead are all located here as well.

CENTRAL AND SOUTHERN COAST

CANAL CREEK
CAMPGROUND

IF YOU'RE LOOKING FOR A QUIET, fairly small, and rather quaint camping area close to the central Oregon Coast but just a few miles from the busy coastal US 101, then Canal Creek is an excellent spot for a night or two.

Canal Creek Campground is located in the lush Siuslaw National Forest. Open all year with easy drive-to access, one could describe it as a "nice little campground." It consists of two circular camping areas. There are 11 drive-in sites in the first section and a large grassy field for open camping in the other section, called the group camping area. It is my understanding that if the group camping area is not reserved, which is often the case, then non-groups can camp there.

Nestled along the base of a ridgeline between two ranges, the lush campground is home to large fern bushes, waxmyrtle, and huckleberry under a canopy of Douglas fir and spruce. True to its name, a very nice 20-foot-wide rippling creek encircles both sections of the camp. In fact, Canal Creek divides one side from the other. No need to fret, though, as Forest Service staff have thought of everything, including a 30 foot walking bridge spanning the creek and connecting the two areas. There is an inconspicuous road through the creek to the group camp, but it is only usable during the drier summer season. During the wet season, there is a waterfall just across the creek opposite site 10.

Each campsite in the first section has drive-in parking, a fire pit, and a picnic table. The group section has fire pits and picnic tables scattered throughout a 300-foot-diameter grassy area. There is a large covered shelter with seating located just over the footbridge near the group camp section. Not surpris-

> *Here's a year-round option in the Siuslaw National Forest with easy access to coastal and wilderness areas.*

RATINGS

Beauty: ✪ ✪ ✪ ✪
Privacy: ✪ ✪ ✪
Spaciousness: ✪ ✪ ✪ ✪
Quiet: ✪ ✪ ✪ ✪
Security: ✪ ✪ ✪
Cleanliness: ✪ ✪ ✪
Insect Control: ✪ ✪

ADDRESS: Canal Creek
Campground
c/o Waldport
Ranger District
P. O. Box 400
Waldport, OR 97394

OPERATED BY: American Land and
Leisure for Suislaw
National Forest

INFORMATION: (541) 547-3679; (877)
444-6777 (toll-free)

OPEN: Year-round

SITES: 11

EACH SITE HAS: Picnic table, fire grill

ASSIGNMENT: First come, first
served; reservations
for group camp only

REGISTRATION: Self-registration on
site

FACILITIES: Vault toilets, hand-
pumped water;
garbage service;
group site with pic-
nic shelter and play
field.

PARKING: At campsites only

FEE: $12

ELEVATION: Sea level

RESTRICTIONS: **Pets:** On leash only
Fires: In fire pits
only
Alcohol: Permitted
Vehicles: Two vehi-
cles per site; small
RVs possible

ingly, given that Camp Creek is a Forest Service campground, there aren't showers, but there are adequate, though not flush, toilets and an old-fashioned hand pump for fresh water— just like at Grandma's. Everybody in the park meets at the water pump sooner or later to exchange (and possibly expand) adventure stories, stir up a little gossip, or maybe even spark a romance. Stranger things have happened . . .

From the coastal town of Waldport on US 101, you need to hang to the left (east) immediately at the south end of the famous Waldport bridge. This puts you on the Alsea Highway. East exactly 7 miles (yep, no more, no less), you will find the sign for Canal Creek Campground with an arrow directing you 4 miles up FS 3462. If you ever wondered what it is like driving around the south island of New Zealand, then this is your road. Nicely paved, though narrow, it winds and winds and winds in a comical back and forth way. With the slow going, you'll have a chance to be impressed with the vast number of bushy green ferns hanging on the sheer ridge wall along the road. Pretty impressive, especially if fern grottoes are your thing.

If you venture out and about on the coast, there is much to do, from beach walks, to fishing, to bay crabbing. For a few bucks, you can have a great afternoon of fun by renting several crab rings with bait and crabbing off the Waldport public pier, located off the Alsea Highway on the east end of town. Only 9 miles south from Waldport on US 101 is the coastal town of Yachats, which is the number one place in the United States for wild mushrooms. Numerous shops and the visitor center have information on great hikes as well as places to look for mushrooms. But remember, if you aren't sure, consider all mushrooms poisonous. The Drift Creek Wilderness is not far from Canal Creek Campground on the north side of Alsea Highway, accessible via FS 3446. This small but wondrous little preserve has claim to the largest stand of old-growth forest remaining in the Coast Range. A must-see, in my estimation.

MAP

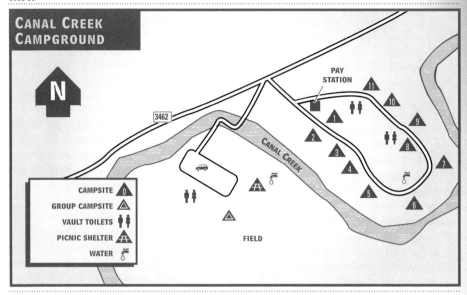

CANAL CREEK CAMPGROUND

N

PAY STATION

3462

CANAL CREEK

CAMPSITE	0
GROUP CAMPSITE	
VAULT TOILETS	
PICNIC SHELTER	
WATER	

FIELD

The Alsea River is most known for steelhead and coho fishing in the winter. It's a good river for beginning and intermediate paddlers, as it has few technical rapids. Log snags can be the most significant hazard, so be on the lookout if you go paddling.

GETTING THERE

From Waldport, on US 101, veer left at the south end of Waldport Bridge onto the Alsea Highway. Continue 7 miles before turning at the campground sign onto FS 3462, the access road. From Albany in the Willamette Valley, head west on US 20 through Corvallis (OR 34 picks up US 20 here) for 15 miles to Philomath. Stay left on OR 34 (Alsea Highway) when it splits from US 20 and continue for 52 very winding miles (most along the Alsea River) to FS 3462. Turn left, Canal Creek is 4 miles in.

CAPE BLANCO STATE PARK CAMPGROUND

> *Cape Blanco happens to be the westernmost point in Oregon and home to the most westerly lighthouse (historic Cape Blanco Light) on the United States mainland.*

WESTWARD TO **US 101** and down the coast, we encounter our second installment in the cape collection (for the others, see pages 11 and 30). While the entire Oregon Coast is one long necklace of windswept headlands and craggy contours linked by a glistening thread of lowland sand dunes and tidal waterways, Capes Blanco, Lookout, and Perpetua are particularly stunning for their natural visual appeal, recreational opportunity, and geologic wonder.

Cape Blanco State Park is the farthest south. The cape, park, reef, lighthouse, airport, and road from US 101 all bear the name Blanco, first given to the dramatic ivory cliffs that rise 200 feet above a black sand beach. In 1603, a relatively unknown Spanish explorer named Martin d'Aguilar spotted the sheer white ("blanco," to him) cliffs and aptly dubbed them for posterity.

This state park covers 1,895 acres of forested headlands and wildflower fields, which flood the area with color in late spring and early summer. Yellow coneflowers, coral bells, yellow sand verbena, and northern dune tansy are the most prevalent varieties. Sitka spruce dominates in the tree department. Farther east in the coastal mountain ranges, one can find old-growth Douglas fir and the commercially prized Port Orford cedar.

The lush vegetation that stays green all year at Cape Blanco (thanks to the temperate marine climate) has been thoughtfully preserved in the campground, lending a certain air of mystery to many of the campsites. If you are lucky enough to snag one that backs up to the ocean, you'll have a thick forest as your buffer for the ultimate in tent-camping privacy. Surprisingly, considering how close the campground sits to the ocean, I didn't notice any with water views. Only two of the cabins are situated to take in any views of the ocean, but it's only a short walk to the bluff for a panoramic vista. In a thick fog, however, make sure you know where the bluff

RATINGS

Beauty: ✿ ✿ ✿ ✿ ✿
Privacy: ✿ ✿ ✿
Spaciousness: ✿ ✿ ✿ ✿
Quiet: ✿ ✿ (summer)
　　　✿ ✿ ✿ ✿ ✿ (winter)
Security: ✿ ✿ ✿ ✿
Cleanliness: ✿ ✿ ✿ ✿ ✿
Insect Control: ✿ ✿ ✿

ends and that unplanned shortcut to the beach starts!
Heavy fog can prevail anytime between late October
and May, but it's between December and February that
the rains make their mark on Cape Blanco—and in generous supply. More than half of the area's total annual
rainfall occurs in this three-month stretch. Summers
(thank heavens) are generally sunny and mild. Temperatures are rarely extremely hot or cold. Shoulder seasons
(March–April and September–October) bring a mixture
of warm, cool, drizzly, breezy, sunny, and cloudy
weather. And that's just in one day!

On a visit to Cape Blanco in late September, I hit a
system that served up cool temperatures and misting
clouds at mid-cape level. Having come from the stifling
heat of the Central Oregon high desert during an
intense and enduring summer fraught with wildfires, it
was actually refreshing to put on a sweater and jacket
for a day or two. If you don't mind waiting five minutes
for the weather to change, the shoulder seasons (otherwise known together as "The Discovery Season" by
Oregon State Parks and Recreation) can be the perfect
time to enjoy a place like Cape Blanco. The summer
tourist season along the Oregon Coast—all 360 miles of
it—is lovely weatherwise, and the scenery is consistently
spectacular, but high season is nevertheless an experience you could learn to hate. There is little relief from
the crowds, campgrounds fill up quickly (including
Cape Blanco, which doesn't require reservations), and
the main north–south route (US 101) is one long, nearly
unbroken procession of RVs and trailers.

But if summer is the only time you can get there,
by all means go. You just have to be a little more cre-
ative to find the pockets of isolation. Joining the seals
offshore in the string of craggy, black basalt outcroppings of Oregon Islands National Wildlife Refuge may
be a bit extreme, however. That's what binoculars are
for. Instead, try the New River paddle route just upcoast
from the park in the town of Denmark. This 8-mile
stretch of tidewater attracts shorebirds and migratory
waterfowl. The New River is a blend of fresh waters
descending from Coast Ranges and the salty Pacific, creating an interesting estuarine mix of plant and animal
life. On one end of the river is undeveloped Floras Lake

KEY INFORMATION

ADDRESS: Cape Blanco State
Park
P.O. Box 1345
Port Orford, OR
97465

OPERATED BY: Oregon State Parks

INFORMATION: (541) 332-6774;
www.oregonstate
parks.org

OPEN: Year-round

SITES: 53; separate
hiker/biker camp

EACH SITE HAS: Picnic table, fire
grill, electricity
(some have shade
trees)

ASSIGNMENT: First come, first
served; no reserva-
tions

REGISTRATION: On site

FACILITIES: Bathhouse with
sinks, toilets, hot
showers; firewood;
laundry; some dis-
abled access; 4
reservable rustic log
cabins, $35; reserv-
able group camp
(30–50 people) and
horse camp

PARKING: At campsites

FEE: $16, $4 hiker/biker,
$8 primitive/over-
flow; $7 per addi-
tional vehicle

ELEVATION: 200 feet

RESTRICTIONS: Pets: On leash only
Fires: In fire pits only
Alcohol: Prohibited
Vehicles: No RV size
limit
Other: 14-day stay
limit

MAP

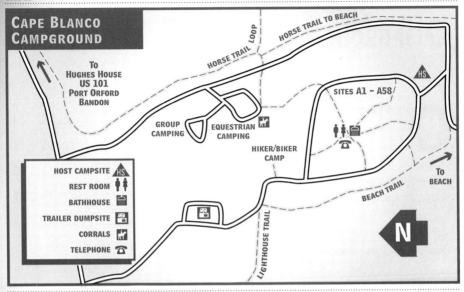

CAPE BLANCO CAMPGROUND

To
HUGHES HOUSE
US 101
PORT ORFORD
BANDON

HORSE TRAIL LOOP

HORSE TRAIL TO BEACH

HORSE TRAIL

SITES A1 – A58

HS

GROUP CAMPING

EQUESTRIAN CAMPING

HIKER/BIKER CAMP

To
BEACH

BEACH TRAIL

LIGHTHOUSE TRAIL

N

HOST CAMPSITE	HS
REST ROOM	
BATHHOUSE	
TRAILER DUMPSITE	
CORRALS	
TELEPHONE	

GETTING THERE

To reach Cape Blanco State Park from Port Orford, drive north on US 101 to Cape Blanco Highway, and then go 5 miles west to the state park campground.

State Park, and at the other end are the sand dunes of Bandon. Both are equally worthy of exploration.

Another alternative is the Sixes River, which forms the northern boundary of Cape Blanco State Park. Fishing in the Sixes is best in the off-season: chinook in the fall, sea-run cutthroat trout in spring and fall, and steelhead in the winter. There are several boat put-ins along the river east of US 101. Hikers can take their pick of varying topographies. A moderate climb up to the windswept bluff near the lighthouse offers views in all directions: north to Blacklock Point and Tower Rock, west across Blanco Reef, and south to Orford Reef. This is an excellent vantage point from which to watch gray whales on their migration path from the Arctic to Baja, California, in winter months.

Down on the beach, you can walk along portions of the Oregon Coast Trail, but keep in mind that tide levels change anywhere from 6 to 12 feet twice daily. The ultimate escape for those experienced enough to handle it is Grassy Knob Wilderness, which lies not far east in a small section of Siskiyou National Forest. Backpacking through this area is best described as bushwhacking; there are very few established trails and the going is steep and rugged.

CAPE PERPETUA SCENIC AREA CAMPGROUND

CAPE PERPETUA, THE LAST of the cape trio, was named by Captain James Cook in 1778. Cook passed by as he fearlessly continued north on his fruitless search for the Pacific link to the Northwest Passage. Both Cape Perpetua and the nearby town of Yachats (pronounced "yah-hots") have long been favored vacation destinations for Oregonians who appreciate the small town's relative seclusion amidst some of the coast's most awe-inspiring scenery. For some unknown reason, Yachats is often overlooked by tourists heading for the bustling centers of Newport and Florence, nearly equidistant to the north and south respectively.

Long before tourists had a road to take them any-where in this vicinity, however, the fog-shrouded seashore and mountain slopes were the domain of coastal Indian tribes, who fished, clammed, and hunted in blissful obscurity. Their contentment was short-lived once the Spanish, English, and Germans discovered the rich resources awaiting exploitation in the area. Along the coast and up nearby verdant river valleys, timber mills, fish canneries, and dairy farms thrived from the late-eighteenth century through the twentieth. While there is still significant activity in these traditional industries, tourism has begun to replace them in the last several decades. Waning resources have forced residents of towns and villages all along the Oregon coast to consider alternative methods of making a living. The transition has not been easy for many of them.

While tourism has only recently seen dramatic growth, the makings for a tourism boom were first put in place in the 1930s with the extension of US 101 and the construction of the first Cape Perpetua Visitor Center by the Civilian Conservation Corps. Today's center is a renovated version of the original, and there is still

> *Cape Perpetua is widely considered to be one of the Oregon coast's most spectacular headlands.*

RATINGS

Beauty: ☆ ☆ ☆ ☆ ☆
Privacy: ☆ ☆
Spaciousness: ☆ ☆ ☆
Quiet: ☆ ☆ ☆ ☆
Security: ☆ ☆ ☆ ☆
Cleanliness: ☆ ☆ ☆ ☆
Insect Control: ☆ ☆ ☆ ☆

ADDRESS: Cape Perpetua
Scenic Area
P.O. Box 274
Yachats, OR 97498

OPERATED BY: American Land and
Leisure for Siuslaw
National Forest

INFORMATION: (541) 563-3211

OPEN: Mid-May to late
September

SITES: 38

EACH SITE HAS: Picnic table, fire grill

ASSIGNMENT: First come, first
served; reservations
and advance deposit
required for group
camp

REGISTRATION: Self-registration on
site

FACILITIES: Flush toilets, piped
water, sanitation sta-
tion, group camp,
public telephone at
visitor center

PARKING: At campsites (back-
in parking recom-
mended)

FEE: $14 Memorial Day
through Labor Day,
otherwise $12;
$6 per additional
vehicle

ELEVATION: Just above sea level

RESTRICTIONS: **Pets:** On leash only
Fires: In fire pits
only
Alcohol: Permitted
Vehicles: RVs up to
22 feet

evidence of the Depression-era workers' housing on the trail between the center and the beach.

The center is a good starting point before taking in the sights of this unique area. As the focal point of the surrounding piece of land known as the Cape Perpetua Scenic Area, the center offers educational exhibits and films as well as a small bookshop. Trails from the center lead off into stands of old-growth spruce in one direction and under the highway to the beach in another. All in all, there are 22 miles of hiking trails within the scenic area. Flanked by state parks on its north and south sides, a wilderness area on the east, the highly photogenic Heceta Head Lighthouse not far south, and the famed Stellar Sea Lion Caves just beyond that, Cape Perpetua Scenic Area has no lack of interesting day trips for visitors based at the campground.

Ah yes, the campground. Cape Perpetua Campground is actually two camping areas within the jurisdiction of the Siuslaw National Forest (as is the rest of the scenic area) but managed by a private contractor, American Lands and Leisure. Both are quite close to the visitor center, and the only difference between them is that one is an individual-site complex and the other accommodates groups of up to 50 people. Privacy at the individual-site campground is less than ideal. To be honest, I contemplated eliminating this entry from the revised book, but after canvassing alternative parks and campgrounds up and down the coast, I decided to stick with Cape Perpetua. Although privacy is painfully lacking because the sites are stretched out along the access road with little vegetation between them, at least they are situated between a creek and a cape so as to give the feeling of being tucked away. Most other campgrounds in the immediate area are sprawling compounds that easily defy description as peaceful.

The campground operates mid-May to late September, but it's worth mentioning that the wild and windswept Cape Perpetua is an enormously popular whale-watching spot in the wintertime. Although the campgrounds are not open, the visitor center has interpretive programs for the whale-watching crowd.

MAP

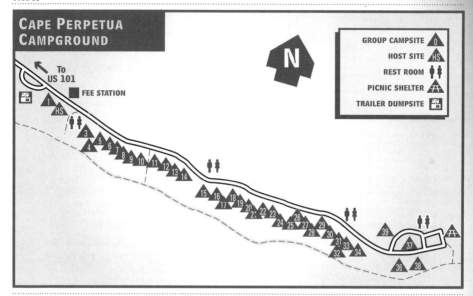

CAPE PERPETUA CAMPGROUND

To US 101

FEE STATION

GROUP CAMPSITE
HOST SITE
REST ROOM
PICNIC SHELTER
TRAILER DUMPSITE

If you want to witness prime examples of the geologic magnificence found at Cape Perpetua Scenic Area close up, stop at Devil's Churn and Captain Cook's Chasm. The relentless movement of sea against basalt rock has formed overhanging cliffs and caves, which are pounded mercilessly at high tides by clashing currents that explode as high as 60 feet into the air. The effect is exhilarating.

All along this portion of the sculpted coast is an endless array of rugged inlets, crescent-shaped coves, and towering capes. Just south of Devil's Churn is the road up to the Cape Perpetua Viewpoint. At 800 feet above the sea, you can have a bird's-eye view of this breathtaking panorama in all directions.

GETTING THERE

To reach Cape Perpetua from Yachats (23 miles south of Newport), drive 3 miles south on US 101. The park entrance is on the non-ocean side.

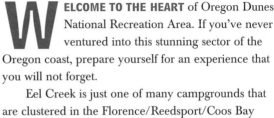

EEL CREEK CAMPGROUND

Backed against some of the largest dunes in Oregon Dunes National Recreation Area, Eel Creek affords a stunning and unforgettable outdoor experience.

WELCOME TO THE HEART of Oregon Dunes National Recreation Area. If you've never ventured into this stunning sector of the Oregon coast, prepare yourself for an experience that you will not forget.

Eel Creek is just one of many campgrounds that are clustered in the Florence/Reedsport/Coos Bay stretch of US 101. Aside from its vegetation-lush private sites, Eel Creek's strongest selling point is the absence of off-road vehicle access to the dunes.

Why these noisy machines are allowed in a place of such serene and fragile beauty is beyond me. Fortunately there are 32,000 acres of sand in Dungeness National Recreation Area, and the jeep trail stops short a mile or two south of Eel Creek, so there's space for everyone here. If you want peace and quiet as part of your dunes experience, however, make sure to avoid hiking in an area where they rent dune buggies.

Eel Creek backs up against some of the largest dunes in the 46-mile-long protected beach. Always shifting, always changing, some dunes that reach as high as 600 feet. Slog your way to the top of one of these monsters and look out over a most spectacular sight—sand, sand, and more sand. Swirled and sculpted in some places, smoothed and glistening like satin in others, rising and falling like patterns of the sea frozen in motion, the pale undulations radiate under a startlingly blue August sky.

The Pacific Ocean is solely responsible for these magnificent mounds, starting some 13,000 years ago when glacial sediment first began the tireless task of forming this section of Oregon's coast. Since then, rivers flowing out of the nearby Coast Range have also contributed their share of deposits. Seasonal patterns of wind and waves combine to add their influence to the sand's destiny, making these the largest collection of

RATINGS

Beauty: ✿ ✿ ✿ ✿ ✿
Privacy: ✿ ✿ ✿ ✿ ✿
Spaciousness: ✿ ✿ ✿ ✿
Quiet: ✿ ✿ ✿ ✿ ✿
Security: ✿ ✿ ✿ ✿
Cleanliness: ✿ ✿ ✿ ✿
Insect Control: ✿ ✿ ✿

active, or "living," coastal sand dunes to be found in America.

Believe it or not, from Eel Creek Campground due west to the ocean is roughly 2 miles. There are places in Oregon Dunes National Recreation Area where the dunes are as much as 3 miles wide—a stiff distance when you're making your way through soft sand. The easiest way to traverse the dunes is along any of the 30 hiking trails within the Recreation Area. It is best to keep to the trails for more noble reasons as well. This is a highly fragile ecosystem, with more than 400 different wildlife species inhabiting the dunes. Of these, 175 are birds.

Headquarters for Oregon Dunes National Recreation Area is right on US 101 at the junction with SR 38 in Reedsport. This is a well-stocked information bureau, with plenty of free guides, brochures, maps, and assorted publications. The exhibits are worth a look, too. It's also a good place to compare notes with other travelers.

As with many other parts of western Oregon, late summer and early fall are prime times, weatherwise, for enjoying the dunes at their best. If it's any indication of winter conditions, Reedsport holds an annual Storm Festival in February. Wind speeds have been clocked as high as 100 miles an hour. Generally, the wind is more problematic than rain. Even in summer, clear skies and warm temperatures are tempered by incessant offshore breezes that often kick up little flurries of sand, which playfully tickle the ankles but can be aggravating at eye level. Sand inside a camera body can be ruinous and costly, so protect your equipment.

Aside from the mesmerizing appeal of the dunes, you'll find a variety of other attractions. The Winchester Bay area offers guided and chartered fishing options, clamming spots too numerous to mention, and a museum and lighthouse. Inland along the Umpqua River is Dean Creek Elk Viewing Area, a 923-acre preserve for free-roaming Roosevelt elk, which are native to the area. The spot also attracts a multitude of waterfowl and migratory birds, including osprey, bald eagles, and blue herons.

KEY INFORMATION

ADDRESS:	Eel Creek Campground Oregon Dunes National Recreation Area 855 Highway 101 Reedsport, OR 97467
OPERATED BY:	Siuslaw National Forest, Oregon Dunes National Recreation Area
INFORMATION:	(541) 271-3611
OPEN:	Mid-May to mid-September
SITES:	52
EACH SITE HAS:	Picnic table, fire grill
ASSIGNMENT:	First come, first served or by reservation in summer at (877) 444-6777 or www.reserveusa.com
REGISTRATION:	Self-registration on site or at camp host
FACILITIES:	Flush toilets, drinking water; boat launch and rentals at nearby Eel Lake
PARKING:	At campsites
FEE:	$13, $7 each additional vehicle
ELEVATION:	Sea level
RESTRICTIONS:	**Pets:** On leash only **Fires:** In fire pits only **Alcohol:** Permitted **Vehicles:** RVs and trailers up to 35 feet

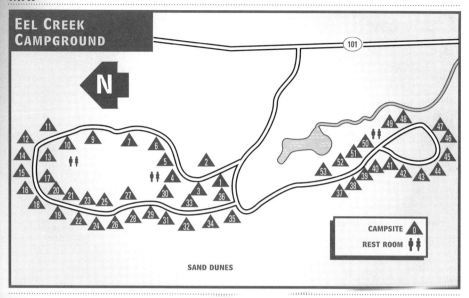

EEL CREEK
CAMPGROUND

N

101

CAMPSITE
REST ROOM

SAND DUNES

GETTING THERE

To get there from Reedsport, drive south on US 101 for 12 miles. The campground entrance is on the ocean side.

It's easy to confuse this campground with Mid Eel, which is only minutes away. Watch for signs to Eel Creek Campground about 12 miles south of Reedsport. The campground is right off US 101 but surprisingly quiet given its close proximity to a busy thoroughfare. Heavy vegetation helps absorb traffic sounds and provides lovely secluded, sandy-bottomed tent sites. Ocean breezes help keep insects to a minimum.

ILLAHE CAMPGROUND

ONE-MILLION-ACRE **SISKIYOU** National Forest contains five designated wild and scenic rivers, the most famous of which is the Rogue. The 35-mile wilderness stretch of the Rogue River is one of the most sought-after whitewater runs in the world, both for the thrill of the whitewater and the incredible scenery through which it travels. The Forest Service wisely uses a lottery permit system to protect the wild Rogue from overuse during the peak season (mid-May through mid-October). You can try to get lucky in the lottery or reserve a spot with a commercial river outfitter to experience the thrills right on (and sometimes in) the rapids.

The Siskiyou also boasts five designated wilderness areas. The Wild Rogue Wilderness is the centerpiece of the 42-mile Rogue River Trail, considered a must-hike by serious trekkers. The trail travels alternately above and beside the river, through contrasting scenery of Douglas fir forests and oak-dotted grasslands. Views of the rapids, waterfalls, river canyon, and wildlife—from otters to black bears to bald eagles and blue herons—abound. Pioneer history comes to life as you view cabins and relics that date to the 1800s.

Just past the wilderness section of the river, a little over a mile from the western end of the Rogue River Trail, lies Illahe Campground. What seems to be a disadvantage of the campground turns out to be its greatest asset. Nearby campgrounds afford easy water access, and thus draw the greater crowds. But at Illahe, where a short, rough trail leads to a rugged shoreline, the relative inaccessibility of the river keeps the crowds away—that is, as long as you don't come between mid-June, when the speedboat racers take over the area, and the end of July. After that, the campers are mostly anglers at play, doing battle with the Rogue's salmon and trout, or winter steelhead come December and

> *Secluded Illahe Campground rests near some of the world's best whitewater runs.*

RATINGS

Beauty: ✰ ✰ ✰ ✰
Privacy: ✰ ✰ ✰ ✰
Spaciousness: ✰ ✰ ✰ ✰
Quiet: ✰ ✰ ✰ (summer)
       ✰ ✰ ✰ ✰ (winter)
Security: ✰ ✰ ✰ ✰ ✰
Cleanliness: ✰ ✰ ✰ ✰ ✰
Insect Control: ✰ ✰ ✰ ✰

KEY INFORMATION

ADDRESS: Illahe Campground
c/o Gold Beach
Ranger District
29279 Ellensburg
Avenue
Gold Beach, OR
97444

OPERATED BY: Siskiyou National
Forest

INFORMATION: (541) 247-3600

OPEN: Year-round

SITES: 14

EACH SITE HAS: Picnic table, fire ring

ASSIGNMENT: First come, first
served; no reservations

REGISTRATION: Self-registration on
site

FACILITIES: Piped water, flush
toilets, sink with mirror, firewood available seasonally; boat
launch and swimming nearby

PARKING: At campsites

FEE: $6, $3 additional
vehicle

ELEVATION: 900 feet

RESTRICTIONS: Pets: On leash only
Fires: In fire pits
only
Alcohol: Permitted
Vehicles: RVs over
22 feet not recommended; no
hookups

January. If hiking is where your interests lie, an outing in the spring or fall will yield the best trail conditions.

Campsites at Illahe have a thick buffer of vegetation that give a feeling of solitude. The area near the campground entrance is grassy and open, dotted with a few apple and plum trees. Campground hosts encourage guests to take the fruit when it ripens, because if the campers don't get it, the bears likely will. (Sensible campers will store food out of sight and out of reach of the critters.) You may catch glimpses of blacktail deer and even wild turkeys here. Cougar sightings have become more common in the area in recent years, to which numerous Forest Service warning posters attest.

Within short reach of Illahe Campground is Foster Bar, where Rogue River floaters take out and revelers swim away the summer heat. From Foster Bar, rafters can be shuttled to a private lodge that abuts Illahe Campground. Shuttle vehicles rarely invade the campground though, and instead use a private road along the river that connects to the lodge.

As you drive along FS 33 toward Illahe, you'll find numerous primitive camping areas that reach the water's edge. About 10 miles south of Illahe Campground, you can turn off FS 33 onto Oak Flat Road, just over the bridge above the Wild and Scenic Illinois River, and travel 3 miles to the Oak Flat dispersed-camping area. For amenities, you'll find a pit toilet and not much else, but you'll be by the water and next to the western trailhead of the 27-mile Illinois River Trail. Like the Rogue River Trail, it is accessible to hikers year-round, but unlike the Rogue Trail (hiking only), the Illinois River Trail allows equestrian, mountain bike, and seasonal motorbike access.

The nearby Myrtle Tree Trail is only half a mile off FS 33, over the Lobster Creek bridge just after the turnoff to the Shrader Trail. It's about half the driving time and half the hiking time of the Shrader Trail, but this unique one-quarter mile path treats visitors to an understory of myrtle trees, instead of the tanoak and madrone that are common to the area. The trail ends at one of the world's largest known myrtle trees, nearly 90 feet tall with a canopy nearly 70 feet wide.

MAP

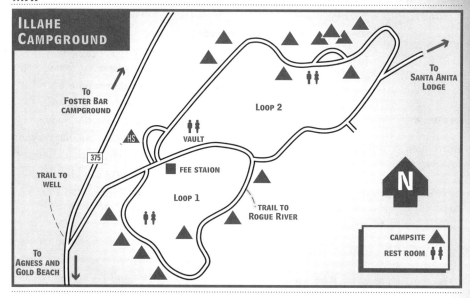

ILLAHE CAMPGROUND

To FOSTER BAR CAMPGROUND

To SANTA ANITA LODGE

LOOP 2

HS

375

VAULT

FEE STAION

TRAIL TO WELL

LOOP 1

TRAIL TO ROGUE RIVER

N

To AGNESS AND GOLD BEACH

CAMPSITE

REST ROOM

Note: As of this writing, the road to Illahe Campground as well as to a number of other campgrounds was closed due to road construction provoked by rock slides in the area. Forest Service roads in this area are gravel and mostly well-graded but pass through some fairly steep and remote terrain. Be advised to check road conditions in advance of your travels in the lower Rogue River region to avoid the disappointment of not being able to arrive as planned. The good news is that there are so many wonderful alternatives in the Siskiyous National Forest that disappointment can quickly become delight with the right adjustment to your itinerary.

GETTING THERE

To reach Illahe from US 101 in Gold Beach, turn east on Jerry's Flat Road north of town and on the south side of the Rogue River. Follow the road, which turns into FS 33, for 35 miles. At the junction after crossing the river, where Agness is left and Powers is straight, veer right on CR 375. In 2 miles, you'll find Illahe Campground on the right. From I-5, exit north of Grants Pass at Merlin-Galice Road. In 16 miles you will come to Galice; go left on FS 23 (Bear Camp Road) for 68 miles of narrow, winding gravel road to FS 33, then proceed as above.

MARYS PEAK
CAMPGROUND

> *This intimate tents-only campground sits at the highest point in Oregon's Coast Range.*

ON A CLEAR DAY, the views from atop Marys Peak are unparalleled. Mount Rainier is visible to the north, Mount Hood to the east, Mount Jefferson to the southeast. The Alsea River, favored by fishermen from the Corvallis/Eugene area for its bountiful steelhead, fall chinook, and coho salmon, fans out to the west with the glistening Pacific beyond. The Alsea is just one of a dozen major rivers sliding out of the Coast Range and into the Pacific.

At 4,097 feet, you are standing on the highest point in the Oregon Coast Range. Sir Edmund Hillary would have to be slightly amused at the modest elevation, but even he could appreciate that undeniable exhilaration of knowing that you are looking down on everything for as far as the eye can see.

Marys Peak (and all of the Coast Range for that matter) sits on ancient basalt that was part of the Pacific Ocean floor some 50 to 60 million years ago. Constant uplifting and shifting of tectonic plates pushes the mountain range ever upward, although the evidence of this activity is not as easily seen on Marys Peak as elsewhere in the range. The dense forest and thick mulchy soil obscure geologic evidence, making this one of the toughest areas for geologists to examine accurately.

If you are familiar with Coast Range weather, you will know that cloudless days on Marys Peak are rare indeed. Siuslaw National Forest, within which Marys Peak is located, is known as a coastal rain forest. That should give you some idea of the degree of wetness that pervades the place. The average annual rainfall in Siuslaw is 90 inches. There are normally as many as 180 days of measurable precipitation annually.

The driest times are late summer and early fall. Don't rule out wintertime, which can actually be quite fun when a substantial snowfall covers the peak and

RATINGS

Beauty: ✿ ✿ ✿ ✿
Privacy: ✿ ✿ ✿
Spaciousness: ✿ ✿ ✿
Quiet: ✿ ✿ ✿ ✿ ✿
Security: ✿ ✿ ✿ ✿
Cleanliness: ✿ ✿ ✿ ✿ ✿
Insect Control: ✿ ✿

makes it an ideal, untracked wonderland for cross-country skiers. The campground is closed from December 1 to March 31, but a Northwest Forest Pass buys you the privilege to park near Connor's Camp and enjoy as much nonmotorized recreation as you can cram into a short winter day.

The same meadows that are cross-country routes in winter are flower-filled delights in the spring. Predominant year-round are the omnipresent evergreens: Douglas, noble, and Pacific silver fir at the higher elevations, with an understory of sword ferns, salal, and oxalis. Stands of western hemlock grow so thickly at lower elevations that the lack of sunshine keeps the underbrush at a low ebb. To help visitors get optimum enjoyment out of the abundant foliage, a quintet of hiking trails offer various rambles around the knobby presence of Marys Peak. They range from the easy, looped Meadowedge Trail that leaves from the campground and to the top of Marys Peak to the moderate 2.4-mile East Ridge Trail through stands of old-growth Douglas fir and Sitka spruce forest to the lengthier North Ridge Trail (5.5 miles) that links Marys Peak with Woods Creek Road down. All in all, 12 miles of trails will take you through two vegetation zones, past old-growth noble fir stands, along the same route once used by sheepherders, and when conditions are right, amongst some of the best wildflower displays in the Coast Range.

Not all flora has enjoyed an untrammeled existence on Marys Peak, however. In the past, the Forest Service allowed disastrous quantities of timber (particularly noble fir) to be cut. A renewed effort is underway to reforest these areas, and Marys Peak Scenic Botanical Area is an experiment to preserve the noble fir and to restimulate its growth. This will not only restore the natural beauty of the area, but also continue to provide habitat for woodland creatures such as deer, grouse, and squirrels.

Sidetrips in the Marys Peak vicinity include the South Fork Alsea River Byway, the Benton County Scenic Loop, William L. Finley National Wildlife Refuge, the Willamette Floodplain, Benton County

KEY INFORMATION

ADDRESS: Marys Peak Campground c/o Waldport Ranger District 1094 SW Pacific Highway (US 101) Waldport, OR 97394

OPERATED BY: Siuslaw National Forest

INFORMATION: (541) 563-3211

OPEN: April through November (varies with seasonal road conditions)

SITES: 6

EACH SITE HAS: Picnic table, fire pit, shade trees

ASSIGNMENT: First come, first served; no reservations

REGISTRATION: Self-registration on site

FACILITIES: Vault toilets

PARKING: At campsites

FEE: $8, $3.50 per additional vehicle

ELEVATION: 4,097 feet

RESTRICTIONS: Pets: On leash only
Fires: In fire pits only
Alcohol: Permitted
Vehicles: No RVs or trailers

MAP

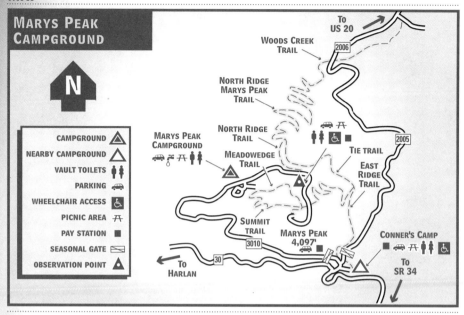

MARYS PEAK CAMPGROUND

N

Legend	
CAMPGROUND	△
NEARBY CAMPGROUND	△
VAULT TOILETS	♀♂
PARKING	🚐
WHEELCHAIR ACCESS	♿
PICNIC AREA	⊼
PAY STATION	■
SEASONAL GATE	⊠
OBSERVATION POINT	▲

To US 20

WOODS CREEK TRAIL — 2006

NORTH RIDGE MARYS PEAK TRAIL

NORTH RIDGE TRAIL — 2005

MARYS PEAK CAMPGROUND

MEADOWEDGE TRAIL

TIE TRAIL

EAST RIDGE TRAIL

SUMMIT TRAIL — 3010

MARYS PEAK 4,097'

CONNER'S CAMP

To SR 34

← To HARLAN — 30

GETTING THERE

To reach Mary's Peak from Philomath (6 miles southwest of Corvallis), follow Alsea Highway (SR 34) southwest for roughly 10 miles to Marys Peak Road (FS 30) and turn right. Follow Marys Peak Road, which becomes FS 3010, to its end and the campground.

Historical Museum in Philomath, Corvallis Arts Center, and Horner Museum, also in Corvallis. There's a nice bike path between Corvallis and Philomath that follows the Willamette and Marys Rivers. Mountain biking on the zillion forest roads in Siuslaw National Forest requires a very good map.

NORTHERN **CASCADES** **AND** ENVIRONS

BADGER LAKE CAMPGROUND

OKAY. CALL ME A MASOCHIST if you want. Perhaps you haven't read enough of this book to know it, but I have to come clean with you on one count: I seem to have a perverse penchant for out-of-the-way campgrounds, some of which nearly require being dropped from above.

Well, Badger Lake Campground is no exception. The last stretch of Forest Road 140 (the third forest road you must navigate) is intended only for high-clearance vehicles. Note that I say "intended." If you drove to Badger Lake right now, you would find normal, low-clearance passenger cars parked there. I don't know how they get there. One of these days, I'm going to ask an intrepid driver. Check for wings, maybe. You certainly can't blame campers who put forth the effort. The campground accommodates tent campers only, many of whom revel in the noticeable lack of RVs. (Please don't tell if an RV manages to make the trip when you visit).

Once upon a time, Badger Lake was accessible only by a steep hike up from a trailhead on SR 35. I'm not entirely sure why (or if) the Forest Service considers its road access an improvement over the trail. You may wonder the same thing as you navigate the rough 10 miles on Forest Service roads from the turnoff at Bennett Pass. A good map may keep you from heading off course onto even worse roads (unimaginable!) but won't help much with the road conditions. Pick up the maps you need at the ranger station in Mount Hood on SR 35 south of Hood River. If you are arriving from the east via the Tygh Valley Road, stop at the Barlow Ranger Station in Dufur for information.

It's a good idea to bring along trail maps too, as area hiking is world-class and the only way to enjoy the rugged scenic beauty of this area. The campground itself sits on the northeast edge of Badger Lake in a

> *Hard to get to and even then accessible only in a high-clearance vehicle, the dramatic beauty of Badger Lake is worth the trouble.*

RATINGS

Beauty: ✪ ✪ ✪ ✪ ✪
Privacy: ✪ ✪ ✪
Spaciousness: ✪ ✪ ✪
Quiet: ✪ ✪ ✪ (summer)
      ✪ ✪ ✪ ✪ ✪ (winter)
Security: ✪ ✪ ✪ ✪ ✪
Cleanliness: ✪ ✪ ✪
Insect control: ✪ ✪

ADDRESS:	Badger Lake Campground c/o Barlow Ranger District 780 NE Court Street Dufur, OR 97021
OPERATED BY:	Mount Hood National Forest
INFORMATION:	(541) 467-2291
OPEN:	July to September
SITES:	4 designated sites; dispersed camping around lake
EACH SITE HAS:	Picnic table, fire grill, shade trees
ASSIGNMENT:	First come, first served; no reservations
REGISTRATION:	Self-registration on site
FACILITIES:	Pit toilets, no piped water
PARKING:	At campsites
FEE:	Northwest Forest Pass required, $5 per day or $30 annually
ELEVATION:	4,472 feet
RESTRICTIONS:	Pets: On leash only Fires: In fire pits only Alcohol: Permitted Vehicles: No RVs or trailers, high-clearance vehicles recommended; non-motorized boats only

nonwilderness corridor adjacent to Badger Creek Wilderness. This is one of Oregon's smaller designated wilderness areas, with only 26,000 acres. But within this tiny (by western protected-land standards) plot are geographic transitions and climatic changes of dramatic proportions unlike those found in any other comparably sized stretch of Oregon topography.

In this unique microcosm, forested mountains meet dusty lowlands across a span of only 12 miles, with nearly 70 inches of precipitation falling annually on the western ridges but only 20 inches in the eastern sector. Old-growth Douglas firs are gradually replaced by the unusual commingling of ponderosa pine and white oak. For some unexplicable reason, these two tree types are found together only in brief stretches along the Columbia River in Washington and along the same longitudinal line between the Hood River and the Dalles in Oregon. Other arboreal examples of the concentrated, transitional diversity are mountain hemlock, lodgepole pine, and Pacific silver fir. Wildlife includes an Audubon count of 150 bird species, as well as deer and elk sightings.

For the best views of this remarkable landscapes (as well as vistas of mighty Mount Hood), hike to the top of 6,525-foot Lookout Mountain. Numerous other trails lead into the backcountry to such destinations as Gumjuwac Saddle, Gunsight Butte, and Flag Point. The Divide Trail between Lookout Mountain and Flag Point looks down on the canyons of Badger Creek for glimpses of dramatic cliffs and rock formations. Wildflowers such as penstemon, Indian paintbrush, and avalanche lily are at their prime in the eastern portion of the wilderness from spring until late July, at which time the colorful displays jump to higher elevations in the west. In total, roughly 80 miles of trails traverse Badger Creek Wilderness, with connecting routes into Mount Hood Wilderness to the north and west.

Located as it is on the eastern slopes of the Cascades at 4,472 feet, Badger Lake and its adjacent trails are usually not snow free until mid-June but stay clear at least through mid-September. Although heavy snow prohibits travel into this high country in winter, Nordic skiers can take advantage of plowed roads from Bennett

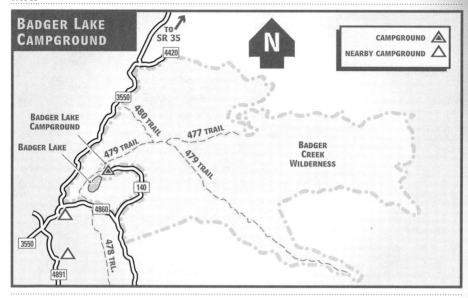

Pass southeast toward the wilderness boundary. SR 35 is kept open all winter to accommodate alpine skiers heading for Mount Hood. Boating on Badger Lake is possible if you didn't lose your canoes on the way in. There's also good rainbow- and brook-trout fishing. The White River Paddle Route farther south along the old Barlow Road (formerly a wagon route for settlers) is another boating option.

The true beauty of Badger Lake Campground is that this remote High Cascade gem is really quite a short drive from metropolitan Portland, making it an easy weekend escape. In less than three hours (factoring in the slowdown on rough roads), you can enjoy a lakeside dinner on a balmy summer evening as you watch the sun sink behind Mount Hood.

GETTING THERE

From the town of Mount Hood (14 miles south of Hood River), travel south on SR 35 for approximately 20 miles to FS 3550. Turn left, and at about 6 miles, turn left onto FS 4860. In 2 miles, turn left again onto FS 140, and follow it to the campground.

BEAVERTAIL CAMPGROUND

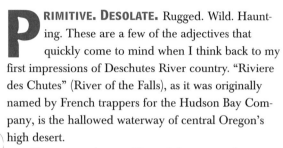

> *This is bare-bones camping at its best: the sky, the sand, the river, and thee. What more could you wish?*

PRIMITIVE. **D**ESOLATE. Rugged. Wild. Haunting. These are a few of the adjectives that quickly come to mind when I think back to my first impressions of Deschutes River country. "Riviere des Chutes" (River of the Falls), as it was originally named by French trappers for the Hudson Bay Company, is the hallowed waterway of central Oregon's high desert.

Flowing north out of Lava Lake just south of Mount Bachelor, the Deschutes (pronounced de shoot) travels toward its confluence with the mighty Columbia River under the protective aegis of state and federal legislation. This is Oregon's second longest river, and its remarkable transformation from docile beginnings above Wickiup Reservoir to a thundering torrent downstream has prompted the separate designations of Upper Deschutes and Lower Deschutes.

Upper Deschutes (from the headwaters to Bend) has been honored with inclusion in the Oregon Scenic Waterway Program for its picturesque, recreational, and natural qualities. Its subtle charms are often overshadowed, however, by its tempestuous lower half, which is the focus of this campground.

The Lower Deschutes River, by far the more popular of the two sections, came under Wild and Scenic River protection in 1988. Its untamed whitewater, steep basalt canyon walls, native trout and steelhead, and historic intrigue attract an eclectic array of recreational users from near and far. The Wild and Scenic status is the river's best insurance that its unspoiled existence will continue indefinitely for all to enjoy.

Today, Beavertail Campground is one of several minimally developed sites along the eastern bank of the Lower Deschutes that are provided in classic Bureau of Land Management style. You've heard the phrase, "less is more?" It could easily be the BLM motto.

RATINGS

Beauty: ☆ ☆ ☆ ☆ ☆
Privacy: ☆ ☆ ☆
Spaciousness: ☆ ☆ ☆
Quiet: ☆ ☆ ☆ (summer)
     ☆ ☆ ☆ ☆ ☆ (winter)
Security: ☆ ☆ ☆ ☆ ☆
Cleanliness: ☆ ☆ ☆
Insect control: ☆ ☆

The Bureau knew what it was doing when it created Beavertail. Views across the water from the riverside compound encompass some of the Lower Deschutes' most spectacular basalt canyon walls. Cedar Island is just downstream, so named for a misplaced stand of incense cedar, which typically grows farther west in the Cascades. So photographers, grab your gear and find a comfortable spot amongst the shore grasses. The kayaks and rafts will be bobbing around the bend any minute.

Speaking of boating, the 51-mile trip from Maupin to the Columbia via the Deschutes requires a permit (available at local outfitters in central Oregon). The BLM Web site is full of information for boaters planning a trip on the Lower Deschutes and uses the word "update" fairly often—this might be a good place to start your trip even before leaving the house. The address is www.or.blm.gov/prineville. Follow the "Recreation" links from there. For experienced paddlers, there are three class IV rapids and dozens of less technical runs for the novices.

One rapid is in a class all by itself. It's known as Sherar's Falls (pronounced shears), and the classification is "portage." The falls are still in use today by the Warm Springs tribe and other local Native Americans who dipnet for trout and spawning salmon from rickety platforms that teeter precariously over the raging spillway below. I watched in awe for nearly an hour one day as a veteran pulled up a fish about every ten minutes and clubbed it senseless with one swift bash of a wooden stick. Lashing the dipnet back into position first, he gutted his catch with lightning speed and carefully packed each in a blanket laden with ice. Except for the ice, this was the same technique practiced for centuries.

The climate in this rugged wildwater backcountry is, as you may have guessed, as extreme as the terrain. Summers can be very hot (in the 90s and 100s), while winters generally drop below freezing. The Bureau of Land Management lands are open all year, so make sure you have all the appropriate emergency supplies depending on your choice of season. Gusty winds and

ADDRESS: Beavertail Campground c/o BLM Prineville District Office P.O. Box 550 Prineville, OR 97754

OPERATED BY: Bureau of Land Management

INFORMATION: (541) 416-6700

OPEN: Year-round

SITES: 15

EACH SITE HAS: Picnic table, grassy tent area, shade trees

ASSIGNMENT: First come, first served; no reservations

REGISTRATION: Self-registration on site

FACILITIES: Vault toilets, hand pumped water, garbage service, wheelchair access, boat launch nearby

PARKING: At campsites

FEE: $8, $2 per additional vehicle; double fees Friday and Saturday

ELEVATION: 2,900 feet

RESTRICTIONS: **Pets:** On leash only **Fires:** In fire pits only, subject to seasonal restrictions **Alcohol:** Permitted **Vehicles:** Driving on vegetation not allowed **Other:** Boating by permit only

MAP

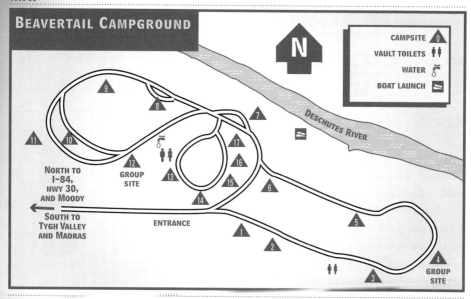

BEAVERTAIL CAMPGROUND

N

CAMPSITE	0
VAULT TOILETS	🚹🚺
WATER	🚰
BOAT LAUNCH	⛵

DESCHUTES RIVER

NORTH TO
I-84,
HWY 30,
AND MOODY

SOUTH TO
TYGH VALLEY
AND MADRAS

GROUP
SITE

ENTRANCE

GROUP
SITE

GETTING THERE

From Maupin (42 miles south of The Dalles on US 197), follow Deschutes River Access Road north along the east bank of the Deschutes River for approximately 21 miles to the campground.

sudden thunderstorms are commonplace. This is a spare campground with the typical scraggly vegetation of the high desert—sagebrush and native grasses predominate riverside. In other words, no towering evergreens to protect you. The car may be the best place to dive if the elements get out of control.

The road that accesses Beavertail and all other BLM dispersed and managed sites is officially known as the Lower Deschutes National Backcountry Byway but is commonly labeled Deschutes River Access Road on maps. This thoroughfare can be quite crowded in summer, especially on weekends. Use caution if you choose to explore by mountain bike. Gravel goes flying as cars careen past.

CAMP CREEK CAMPGROUND

Zigzag

TIRED OF DRIVING FOREVER on rough forest roads just to find a place to set up camp? Then check out Camp Creek. You can't beat the convenience of this campground, located directly off US 26 right in the heart of the Mount Hood National Forest.

While the campground itself doesn't have supplies (except firewood, which you can buy from the camp host), it's a short distance to the small mountain towns of Zigzag and Government Camp. You won't even realize that you're a stone's throw away from civilization once you set up your tent at one of the creekside sites, which provide white noise as a pleasant, natural backdrop. The shade of the Douglas fir trees and the rushing creek give you the feeling of having gotten away from it all. Although, as with many of the area campgrounds, it tends to get a little crowded, the beauty of Camp Creek Campground is that the sites are relatively spacious, so you won't feel like you're on top of your neighbor. In one of our favorite sites, there is a seat carved out of a tree trunk so you can enjoy a private view of the moon lighting up the creek below.

Only 20 miles east of Portland, Mount Hood National Forest totals 1,067,043 acres, of which 189,200 are in designated wilderness areas. Mount Hood Wilderness, the largest, encompasses the summit and upper slopes of its namesake peak. The forest is laced with hiking trails, many within a few miles of Camp Creek. Fishing, berry-picking, bird-watching, bicycling, and mushroom-hunting are also popular activities in the area.

Hidden Lake Trail, the longest major trail within Mount Hood Wilderness, departs from a trailhead off FS 2639 (Kiwanis Camp Road), which intersects OR 26 5 miles east of the hamlet of Rhododendron. Along the path you'll spot many of the flowering shrubs for which the town is named (blossoming in profusion in

> *Conveniently located off the highway, this campground is a great place for a quick getaway to the Mount Hood area.*

RATINGS

Beauty: ✪ ✪ ✪ ✪
Privacy: ✪ ✪ ✪
Spaciousness: ✪ ✪ ✪
Quiet: ✪ ✪ ✪
Security: ✪ ✪ ✪
Cleanliness: ✪ ✪ ✪ ✪
Insect control: ✪ ✪ ✪ ✪

ADDRESS: Camp Creek
Campground
c/o Mount Hood
Information Center
65000 East US 26
Welches, OR 97067

OPERATED BY: Mount Hood
National Forest

INFORMATION: (503) 622-7674,
(888) 622-4822

OPEN: Mid-April through
early October

SITES: 25

EACH SITE HAS: Picnic table, fire ring

ASSIGNMENT: First come, first
served or by reser-
vation at (877)444-
6777 or www.reserve
america.com

REGISTRATION: With camp host

FACILITIES: Hand-pumped
water, vault toilets,
firewood for sale

PARKING: At campsites only

FEE: $14, $7 per additional vehicle

ELEVATION: 2,200 feet

RESTRICTIONS: **Pets:** On leash only
Fires: In fire rings
only
Alcohol: Permitted
at campsites only
Vehicles: 22-foot RV
size limit

June) as you ascend to a forested lake. A round-trip to the terminus (beyond the lake) totals 10 miles. The easier 0.6-mile Little Zigzag Falls Trail also departs from FS 2639 to follow Little Zigzag Creek to its namesake falls. You can get the latest area trail information by visiting www.fs.fed.us/r6/mthood/recreation/trails/zigzag-conditions.shtml, which will give you details on snow conditions, recent trail maintenance, and permit requirements.

The Zigzag Ranger District also sponsors several wildflower hikes during the summer. The popular Top Spur Trail leads through flower-cloaked meadows to the crest of Bald Mountain, and the Trillium Lake Trail traverses colorful fields at the water's edge. Contact the district at (503) 622-3191 for guided-hike schedules and for additional information on Mount Hood's many trails. Note that trailhead parking requires a Northwest Forest Pass ($5 per day or $30 annually).

If you want close-up view of the 11, 237-foot Mount Hood, Oregon's tallest mountain, take the 6-mile winding drive up to Timberline Lodge, which sits midway up the summit of the mountain and offers restaurants and hiking trails with a great view of the mountain. A true resting volcano, Mount Hood is a popular mountain-climbing destination. If you have the moxy (and the legs and lungs), a climb to Hood's summit is the adventure of a lifetime. A wilderness permit is required of all persons attempting the ascent.

Overall, Camp Creek is a great base camp for anything you might want to do in the Mount Hood area, and with its convenience combined with great scenery, it's one of the tops in this popular region. Consequently, you may want to reserve a creekside site if you plan to go on a holiday weekend, or any sunny summer weekend for that matter, as those are the best plots of the bunch.

MAP

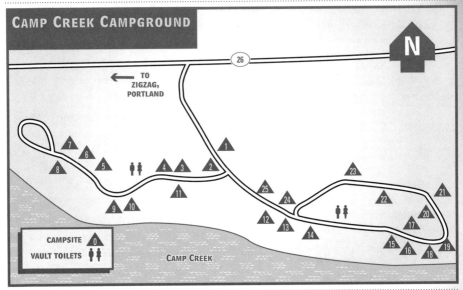

CAMP CREEK CAMPGROUND

N

26

← TO ZIGZAG, PORTLAND

CAMPSITE ▲

VAULT TOILETS

CAMP CREEK

GETTING THERE

From Portland, drive east on US 26 for 35 miles to Zigzag. Continue through Zigzag and drive 4 miles to the campground on the right-hand side of the highway.

EAGLE CREEK
CAMPGROUND

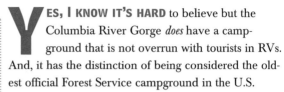

> *If you're cruising along I-84 to Portland beside the Columbia River and you've just about given up on finding a campground not swarming with RVs, all is not lost.*

YES, **I** KNOW IT'S HARD to believe but the Columbia River Gorge *does* have a campground that is not overrun with tourists in RVs. And, it has the distinction of being considered the oldest official Forest Service campground in the U.S.

Built in 1915, Eagle Creek Campground is perched above the Columbia River and the very busy I-84 corridor in a rustic setting that has changed little since it first opened. Then, Eagle Creek sported amenities that must have been talked about from Portland to Pendleton: flush toilets that are still in use today!

Eagle Creek is quite a pleasant surprise, whether you plan a sojourn high into the backcountry of the Columbia Wildnerness or just need a shady afternoon respite from the freeway below. Situated within the Columbia River Gorge National Scenic Area (headquartered in Hood River 20 miles east), the campground lies just east of the Bonneville Dam almost equidistant between the towns of Bonneville and Cascade Locks. It's easy to miss the turnoff, and it's hard to slow down, too. Everyone drives like a bat out of hell on I-84—except, of course, for the occasional boardhead bound for a little windsurfing in Hood River sputtering along in (you guessed it) a battered Volkswagen minibus.

Once you're off the freeway with car and nerves intact, nose through the lower parking area and follow the camp road up through towering true fir, western red cedar, and hemlock trees to the campground. The busy freeway teeming with tourists and those intractable tractor-trailers will quickly fade into oblivion, if only temporarily. You'll be surprised at how remote you feel in just a few minutes!

Despite this sense of isolation at the campground, if you've come to hike the trails, you probably won't be alone. Trails throughout the Eagle Creek basin and

RATINGS

Beauty: ✿ ✿ ✿ ✿
Privacy: ✿ ✿ ✿ ✿
Spaciousness: ✿ ✿ ✿
Quiet: ✿ ✿ ✿ (summer)
    ✿ ✿ ✿ ✿ ✿ (winter)
Security: ✿ ✿ ✿
Cleanliness: ✿ ✿ ✿ ✿
Insect control: ✿ ✿ ✿

up into the Columbia Wilderness are some of the most popular in the Columbia River Gorge. But the main trail has many spurs that can be traversed to and fro or combined with other trails to create loop trips. There is a network of more than 90 trail miles within the Columbia Wilderness (including 14 of the Pacific Crest Trail alone), so you're bound to find some solitude if you have time to wander. While there are varying trail lengths to accommodate all skill levels, it should be noted that the preponderance involve respectable elevation gains, with beginning points starting just above sea level and destination lakes, ridges and plateaus topping out around 4,000 feet.

The historic Eagle Creek Trail, also built in 1915, is an example of a long, gradual ascension, with 13 miles that parallel Eagle Creek up to Wahtum Lake. Along the way, the trail passes high cliffs along Eagle Creek and oodles of waterfalls (Punchbowl Falls being the most notable), then crests atop the broad plateau of Waucoma Ridge, which looks out over the expansive Columbia River Gorge and south to Mount Hood. Ruckel Creek Trail, on the other hand, just east of the campground via a short connector trail, is a rigorous 6-mile climb nearly straight up to Benson Plateau for 3,700 feet of elevation gain.

Two loop trips—one shorter, one ambitious—incorporate stretches of the Pacific Crest Trail, which crosses the Columbia River at the Bridge of the Gods (a worthy sidetrip of its own) and passes through the wilderness to its boundary at Wahtum Lake. Ask park staff for directions and details. For the most accurate picture of the trail system within Columbia Wilderness and to find hikes that suit your comfort level, check with the Mount Hood National Forest headquarters in Sandy.

Weatherwise, this is an area of transition between moisture-laden western Oregon and the more arid climes in the east. The Gorge itself adds its own wind-tunnel effect, so prepare for variety even in summer. Thunderstorms materialize quickly, and the wind can blow hard, particularly in late afternoon. In fact, the Columbia River has achieved an international reputation among sailboarders for this exact reason. The discovery has transformed the burg of Hood River, once

KEY INFORMATION

ADDRESS: Eagle Creek Campground c/o Columbia River Gorge National Scenic Area 902 Wasco Avenue, Suite 200 Hood River, OR 97031

OPERATED BY: Columbia River Gorge National Scenic Area

INFORMATION: (541) 386-2333

OPEN: Mid-May to October

SITES: 20

EACH SITE HAS: Picnic table, fire pit with grill

ASSIGNMENT: First come, first served; no reservation

REGISTRATION: Self-registration on site

FACILITIES: Bathhouse with flush toilets and piped water (no showers)

PARKING: At campsites

FEE: $10

ELEVATION: Sea level

RESTRICTIONS: **Pets:** On leash only **Fires:** In fire grates only **Alcohol:** Permitted **Vehicles:** 22-foot RV and trailer size limit, no hookups

MAP

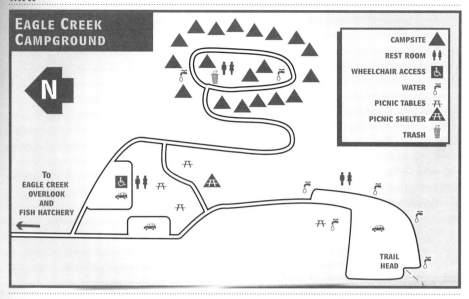

EAGLE CREEK CAMPGROUND

N

To
EAGLE CREEK
OVERLOOK
AND
FISH HATCHERY

CAMPSITE	▲
REST ROOM	🚻
WHEELCHAIR ACCESS	♿
WATER	🚰
PICNIC TABLES	⛩
PICNIC SHELTER	⛺
TRASH	🗑

TRAIL
HEAD

GETTING THERE

From Portland, drive 41 miles east on I-84 to Exit 41 (2 miles past the town of Bonneville). From the east on I-84, there is no westbound exit, so continue on for 2 miles to Exit 40, Bonnevile Dam, and return to the interstate eastbound to Exit 41. At the stop sign, turn right and follow signs to Eagle Creek. You'll come first to a lower day-use parking area, but continue up the winding road through the forest to the campground.

a quiet farming and fishing community, into a veritable Mecca of sailboard mania, with renovated hotels, bed-and-breakfasts, trendy shops, espresso bars, micro-breweries, and cafes catering to a transient population that literally comes and goes with the wind.

Long before the windsurfers, Native Americans were the first to pay homage to the winds of the Columbia. Lewis and Clark were the first white explorers to use the river as a highway, opening the door to continued use by settlers who, at The Dalles, traded Conestoga wagons for the steamboats that carried them to their new homes in the Northwest territory. Rapids and falls that had to be portaged then no longer exist today because the wild and mighty flow of the Columbia was harnessed by power companies in the twentieth century.

For those curious about the hydroelectric business and wanting a respite from outdoor activities, the Bonneville Dam gives tours daily. Other points of interest nearby—both indoors and out—include Cascade Locks, Crown Point Vista House and Observatory, Multnomah Falls and Multnomah Falls Lodge, Bridal Veil Falls, and Fort Dalles Museum.

ELK LAKE CAMPGROUND

THE WORD FOOLHARDY may come to mind as you find yourself at the junction that leads to this gem of a camping spot in Willamette National Forest, about 10 miles above the small, historic burg of Detroit.

"Rough Road" is the more-than-understated message on the sign that the Forest Service has (jokingly, perhaps?) placed at the intersection of FS 4696 and FS 4697. The road is decidedly rough but, we found, not impassable if you hold onto your teeth and don't exceed 5 miles an hour. As long as your exhaust system and oil pan sit high and secure, you should be okay.

Hugging the southern boundary of Bull of the Woods Wilderness, peaceful Elk Lake is aptly named for the huge herds of elk that once grazed in this area. It lies in the subalpine shadow of Battle Ax Mountain, Mount Beachie, and Gold Butte and is a classic Cascade escape that probably remains so because the Forest Service insists on not improving the access road. (Perhaps the ill maintenance is intentional, but on the other hand, it may be a matter of funds.) Elk Lake Campground sits at the western tip of this peanut-shaped lake and is accessible by following the road along the north side of the lake to the short spur that drops down off the main road to the left.

Elk Lake's campsites are strung along the shore of the lake. Tall stands of Douglas fir and western hemlock share the land with white fir, birches, Oregon grape, ferns, and trillium to offer a prime collection of natural cover. In early July, pink-blossomed rhododendrons seem somehow out of place in this rugged, woodsy setting.

This campground may be tough to get to, but once you're there, it makes for a terrific base camp while you enjoy the region's recreational options. At the top of the list is hiking into Bull of the Woods

> *Beware: The road in is rough with a capital R. But once there, you'll find this is a great base camp for exploring Willamette National Forest and two wilderness areas.*

RATINGS

Beauty: ✿ ✿ ✿ ✿ ✿
Privacy: ✿ ✿ ✿ ✿
Spaciousness: ✿ ✿ ✿ ✿ ✿
Quiet: ✿ ✿ ✿ ✿ ✿
Security: ✿ ✿ ✿
Cleanliness: ✿ ✿ ✿ ✿
Insect Control: ✿ ✿ ✿

ADDRESS: Elk Lake
Campground
c/o Detroit Ranger
District
HC 73, Box 320
Mill City, OR 97360

OPERATED BY: Willamette National
Forest

INFORMATION: (503) 854-3366

OPEN: July to late September

SITES: 14

EACH SITE HAS: Picnic table, fire pit
with grill, shade
trees

ASSIGNMENT: First come,
first serve; no
reservations

REGISTRATION: Not necessary

FACILITIES: Pit toilets, primitive
boat launch; no
piped water and no
garbage service
(pack out all
garbage)

PARKING: At campsites and
and in general park-
ing area (a short
walk to some camp-
sites); four-wheel
drive recommended

FEE: None

ELEVATION: 4,000 feet

RESTRICTIONS: Pets: On leash only
Fires: In fire pits
only
Alcohol: Permitted
Vehicles: Not recom-
mended for low-
clearance vehicles

Wilderness, which is home to one of western Oregon's few remaining old-growth forests. From Beachie Saddle (about a mile west of the campground on FS 4697), trailheads strike out for Battle Ax Mountain to the north (into the wilderness) and Mount Beachie to the south. This section of FS 4697 is not recommended for any motor vehicles; consider this a warm-up for the steep 2-mile and 1.5-mile grunts up Battle Ax and Beachie, respectively. You will be greeted, however, by views that are well worth the effort. A less strenuous hike follows Elk Lake Creek northeast into Bull of the Woods Wilderness from a trailhead near where the creek feeds its namesake. For extended trips into the wilderness backcountry, take the trail that leaves very near the campground spur road. In 1998, a sizeable chuck of Bull of the Woods Wilderness was annexed to help create adjoining Opal Creek Wilderness, so be sure you have a current map of the area showing both areas.

If you are thinking Elk Lake might be a nice spot to take in lazy kayaking or canoeing, you're right. Anyone foolhardy enough to drag a boat into this remote locale deserves to be rewarded (or psychoanalyzed). An undeveloped put-in accommodates inflatable rafts, kayaks, canoes, and other small, nonmotorized craft. Pick up a fishing permit at the general store in Detroit if you have thoughts of angling for your dinner. For either boating or fishing, don't overlook little Dunlap Lake (named for an early prospector), which is hidden from view about a mile before you get to Elk Lake. Forest Service roads also await exploration if you have the foresight to bring your mountain bike along. Test your skill downhill on the 2-mile "riverbed" and pedal on up FS 4696 (to the left) to Gold Butte. The views of mountain peaks from this formerly manned fire lookout are staggering on a clear day—north to Mount Hood, east to Mount Jefferson, south to Mount Washington. Farther up FS 46 is Breitenbush Hot Springs, worth a dip for tired muscles.

Note: After speaking with the Detroit Ranger Station and decided to retain this entry in the book because this is such a beautiful and remote area. However, be aware that the road has only gotten

MAP

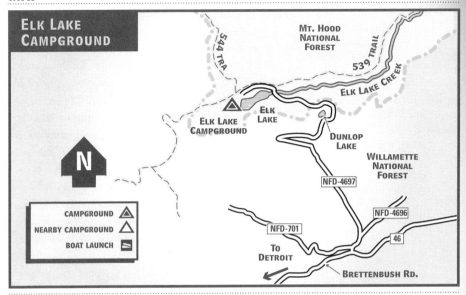

worse (if that's possible), with no plans to improve it, and the campsites have essentially deteriorated into dispersed areas. There are, however, plans to improve the toilets (not sure of the logic here) in 2004. I can't bring myself to eliminate this spot from the book, but if you go, you can't say I didn't warn you.

GETTING THERE

To reach Elk Lake Campground from Detroit (50 miles southeast of Salem), drive north on FS 46 (Breitenbush Road) for 4.5 miles to FS 4697. Turn left and continue for 10 miles to the campground. Stay to the left fork where FS 4697 and FS 4696 intersect at about 8 miles. The last 2 miles are extremely rough.

ELKHORN VALLEY CAMPGROUND

> *This is minimalist camping at its best in a heavily forested compound along the Little North Santiam River.*

I AM NOT AT ALL ASHAMED to admit that I had an ulterior motive when I was planning to visit Elkhorn Valley Recreation Site. You see, there's this golf course I'd read about . . .

For years, I'd heard about a nine-hole track (a second nine opened in 2000) east of Salem that had gained national recognition for its outstanding natural setting and challenging layout. Being above-average in my passion for the game (there are those who will say crazy), I cleverly crafted an itinerary that put me in the neighborhood. I figured a golf game would be an excellent antidote to the camping overdose and allow me to stretch my road-weary limbs.

I soon discovered that showing up at Elkhorn Valley Golf Course as a single on a brilliant Sunday morning in the summertime is more foolhardy than hoping to find a campground free of RVs.

Sulking back to my car, I was downright irritated to have my perfect plan botched. I sat on the tailgate, drinking cold coffee and eating a stale donut, contemplating my options. I watched enviously as foursome after foursome with tee times pulled into the parking lot, making way too much noise for a breathless summer morning and talking that pre-round talk: "I've got 75 in my bones today, boys, so just give me your money now and it will seem a whole lot less painful later on."

That was enough for me. Off to Elkhorn Valley Recreation Site I went, and what a treat that was! Who needs golf, anyway?

Nestled along the Little North Santiam River under dense stands of old growth, Elkhorn Valley Recreation Site has the feel of a campground much farther removed from the urban pace than one would expect within 35 easy miles of metropolitan Salem. The North Fork Road in from OR 22 is paved all the

RATINGS

Beauty: ☆ ☆ ☆ ☆ ☆
Privacy: ☆ ☆ ☆ ☆
Spaciousness: ☆ ☆ ☆ ☆ ☆
Quiet: ☆ ☆ ☆ ☆
Security: ☆ ☆ ☆ ☆ ☆
Cleanliness: ☆ ☆ ☆ ☆ ☆
Cleanliness: ☆ ☆

way (although there are a surprising number of dips and twists to keep inattentive drivers alert). Within minutes of the turn to the northeast along the Elkhorn Valley corridor, the weekend escapist is treated to a deep green enclave that immediately soothes the spirit.

Designed in standard minimalist Bureau of Land Management style, Elkhorn Valley has 24 campsites simply staged in three generously-spaced clusters, areas A, B and D—not sure what happened to C. It's hard to say which area is best; chances are you'll take whatever you can get if it's a busy summer weekend, as availability is first come, first served. Area A has the most sites (10) and is situated closest to the North Fork Road where it passes by above. I found these sites to be the most closely spaced. Area D is at the end of the camp road, affording the greatest sense of being tucked into the forest, but this is also a turnaround point for campers heading back out, and has the potential for traffic clogs. Sites in area B are closest to the river and are set up in more of a walk-in fashion. The best site of all may be 26, which sits by itself on the river at the end of the camp road.

For the most part, each site and parking space is positioned in such a way so as not to unduly infringe upon neighboring sites. Each comes with picnic table and fire pit. Unlike most compounds of this relatively intimate nature, each cluster has its own pay station and restroom for true self-sufficiency. There's a Rim Trail that runs the entire ridge above the three areas and a River Trail between areas B and D. A spur trail connects the Rim Trail to the River Trail via a handy boardwalk and footbridge elevated above the soggy lowland behind area D.

You don't have to go far to enjoy spectacular scenery in Elkhorn Valley. While the campground's primeval forest setting may be enough for you, a short drive further up the North Fork Road past Elkhorn Valley Golf Course and Shady Grove Campground puts you at the access point for the Opal Creek Wilderness, a fairly recent addition to Oregon's wilderness collection designated in 1998. The Opal Creek Scenic Recreation Area designation came even more recently in 2002.

KEY INFORMATION

ADDRESS: Elkhorn Valley Campground c/o Tillamook Resource Area Salem District Office 1717 Fabry Road SE Salem, OR 97306

OPERATED BY: Bureau of Land Management

INFORMATION: (503) 375-5646

OPEN: Mid-May to late September

SITES: 24

EACH SITE HAS: Picnic table, fire grill

ASSIGNMENT: First-come, first-served; no reservations

REGISTRATION: Self-registration on site

FACILITIES: Vault toilets, hand-pumped water, picnic area, firewood available for purchase, garbage service, river access, trails, camp host

PARKING: At campsites

FEE: $10, $5 per additional vehicle

ELEVATION: 1,200 feet

RESTRICTIONS: Pets: On leash only
Fires: In fire pits only
Alcohol: Permitted
Vehicles: Large trailers not recommended
Other: 14-day stay limit; no gathered wood more than 1" in diameter; gate closed at 10pm

MAP

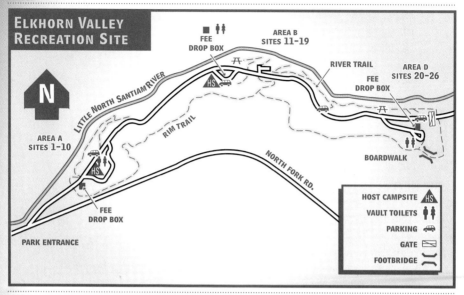

ELKHORN VALLEY RECREATION SITE

N

LITTLE NORTH SANTIAM RIVER

FEE DROP BOX

AREA B
SITES 11-19

RIVER TRAIL

AREA D
SITES 20-26

FEE DROP BOX

AREA A
SITES 1-10

RIM TRAIL

NORTH FORK RD.

BOARDWALK

FEE DROP BOX

PARK ENTRANCE

HOST CAMPSITE   HS
VAULT TOILETS
PARKING
GATE
FOOTBRIDGE

GETTING THERE

From Salem, drive 28 miles east on OR 22 towards Detroit. At Lyons, turn left onto North Fork Road and drive 9 miles to the campground on the left. You'll pass Canyon Creek Day-Use Area on the way.

This small but notable wilderness tract is home to two wild and scenic rivers (Opal Creek and Elkhorn Creek). Just as importantly, it protects some of the last great old-growth trees of the Willamette Valley, with one Douglas fir in particular on the trail to Opal Pool known to be 1,000 years old. It is not uncommon to pass stands of trees on various other trails in the Opal Creek Wilderness with specimens easily between 500 and 750 years old. Take your pick of several lowland or highland hikes that also take in views of waterfalls, crystal clear pools, and rugged mountain peaks.

The lands in the Elkhorn Valley corridor are operated under a sometimes-confusing conglomeration of state forest, national forest, and BLM jurisdiction. It's best to contact the BLM or Willamette National Forest for a good overview map of the area.

HOOVER CAMPGROUND

DETROIT, OREGON, HAS a peculiar namesake, considering it's not anything like the Motor City—it's a small town (about 300 people live here) with cute shops and restaurants right on OR 22. There are plenty of campgrounds in the Detroit Lake area, and Hoover campground is one of the best. For starters, they have some of the friendliest camp hosts around, so if you're camping solo you'll feel secure knowing that someone is looking out for you.

All along OR 22, you'll see signs pointing you to different trails in the area, so you can pick your pleasure (the Detroit Ranger Station is also nearby, where you can pick up a map and get trail suggestions). Stahlman Point Trail, right off the entrance road, will take you to a stellar, sweeping lookout over Detroit Lake. The lake itself is also popular for fishing, swimming, picnicking, boating, even waterskiing, and its day-use area is close to the campground. Anglers and boaters can also cast and put-in on the North Santiam River, which abuts the campground.

The campground is small but loaded with amenities such as flush toilets, boat launch, picnic tables, fire rings, water, and garbage service. However, there are no hookups at any of the 37 sites, making this campground less appealing to big RVs. Next to the campground is the Hoover Day-Use Area, where you'll find the boat launch and access to fishing and swimming. Aside from individual sites, Hoover Campground hosts a group campsite that accommodates up to 70 people.

The campground is located within the Willamette National Forest, which is home to seven volcanic peaks: Mount Jefferson, Three Fingered Jack, Mount Washington, the Three Sisters (North, Middle, and South), and Diamond Peak. Packed with scenic peaks and pristine rivers, Willamette National Forest is 110 miles long and covers 1.6 million acres. It is easily

> *Pleasant Hoover Campground is convenient to Detroit Lake and the trail system of the Willamette National Forest.*

RATINGS

Beauty: ✿ ✿ ✿
Privacy: ✿ ✿ ✿
Spaciousness: ✿ ✿ ✿
Quiet: ✿ ✿ ✿
Security: ✿ ✿ ✿ ✿
Cleanliness: ✿ ✿ ✿ ✿
Insect control: ✿ ✿ ✿

ADDRESS: Hoover Campground
c/o Santiam
P.O. Box 561
Detroit, OR 97342

OPERATED BY: Santiam Recreation
for Willamette
National Forest

INFORMATION: (503) 854-3366

OPEN: April through
September

SITES: 37

EACH SITE HAS: Picnic table, fire ring

ASSIGNMENT: First come,
first served; no reser-
vations

REGISTRATION: With camp host

FACILITIES: Flush toilets, firewood for sale, water
spigots, amphithe-
ater, boat launch,
wheelchair-accessible
fishing pier

PARKING: At campsites only

FEE: $12, $5 per additional vehicle

ELEVATION: 1,600 feet

RESTRICTIONS: **Pets:** On leash only
Fires: In fire rings
only
Alcohol: Permitted
at campsites only
Vehicles: 30-foot RV
size limit, no
hookups
Other: 14-day stay
limit

accessed via four major highways and convenient to tent campers living in western or central Oregon. In addition to breathtaking vistas, the flora of Willamette is worth the visit alone. Centuries-old Douglas fir and western red cedar combine with other forest beauties such as spruce and hemlock to weave an astounding canopy over this rough, glaciated landscape.

Although many trails in this area are conveniently located right off the highway, you can also access some in the backcountry if you don't mind driving off-road a little; nearby Coffin Mountain is one of my favorite hiking areas, but be prepared for a long, bumpy drive to the trailhead.

The Coffin Mountain trail network includes the 1.7-mile Bruno Meadows Trail, which wanders beneath mature Douglas and Noble firs and past a rocky out-cropping that affords views of a wildflower-clad meadow. It intersects the 2.5-mile Bugaboo Ridge Trail for access to the 1.9-mile Bachelor Mountain Trail, which offers sweeping vistas of the Cascades. By plac-ing a shuttle vehicle at the Bachelor Mountain trail-head, you can explore the region without backtracking. For a shorter outing but plenty of exercise, tackle the 1.5-mile Coffin Lookout Trail, which ascends 1,000 feet to a fire lookout, staffed in the summer, with views of Coffin Mountain and Buck Creek Valley below.

For those who like to know that conveniences are nearby, Detroit is stocked with stores, coffee shops, and gas stations with friendly faces behind the coun-ters. Although the area can get crowded on a sunny summer weekend, the amount of campgrounds in the region means you're likely to be able to find a last-minute spot to set up camp.

MAP

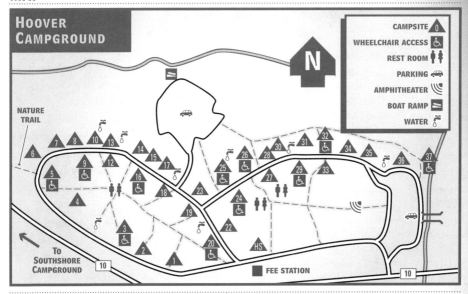

HOOVER CAMPGROUND

CAMPSITE △
WHEELCHAIR ACCESS ♿
REST ROOM 🚻
PARKING 🚐
AMPHITHEATER 🔊
BOAT RAMP ⛴
WATER ⚱

NATURE TRAIL

To
SOUTHSHORE
CAMPGROUND

10

FEE STATION

10

GETTING THERE

From Detroit (about 50 miles east of Salem on OR 22), drive east on OR 22 to Blowout Road (FS 10). Turn right and continue 4 miles to the campground on the right.

OXBOW
REGIONAL PARK
CAMPGROUND

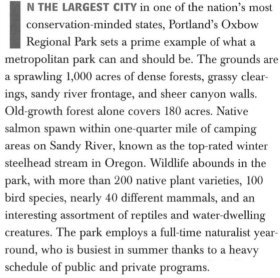

> *An easy 20 miles from downtown Portland, Oxbow Regional Park is an amazing blend of recreational diversity, scenic delight, and environmental consciousness.*

IN THE LARGEST CITY in one of the nation's most conservation-minded states, Portland's Oxbow Regional Park sets a prime example of what a metropolitan park can and should be. The grounds are a sprawling 1,000 acres of dense forests, grassy clearings, sandy river frontage, and sheer canyon walls. Old-growth forest alone covers 180 acres. Native salmon spawn within one-quarter mile of camping areas on Sandy River, known as the top-rated winter steelhead stream in Oregon. Wildlife abounds in the park, with more than 200 native plant varieties, 100 bird species, nearly 40 different mammals, and an interesting assortment of reptiles and water-dwelling creatures. The park employs a full-time naturalist year-round, who is busiest in summer thanks to a heavy schedule of public and private programs.

There have been a number of upgrades made to the park since the publication of this guidebook's predecessor. Now, campers enjoy a choice of more campsites (22 have been added for a total of 67) and two new restrooms, with the ultimate in camping comfort: Flush toilets arrived at Oxbow along with hot showers, heated bathroom floors, and hot-air hand dryers. It's almost better than home—but still with all the other rustic charms and natural beauty that make this such a great park.

You'll have a hard time deciding what to do first once you've set up camp. And do that as soon as you arrive. Sites are first-come, first-served, although it would be hard to find a bad spot. The park staff has been busy improving the privacy between sites with natural vegetation and cedar fences. It's music to the ears of tent campers everywhere when peace and quiet become a priority.

The first order of business after finding your spot may be to explore the trails on foot. There are roughly

RATINGS

Beauty: ✰ ✰ ✰ ✰ ✰
Privacy: ✰ ✰ ✰ ✰
Spaciousness: ✰ ✰ ✰ ✰
Quiet: ✰ ✰ ✰ ✰
Security: ✰ ✰ ✰ ✰ ✰
Cleanliness: ✰ ✰ ✰ ✰
Insect control: ✰ ✰ ✰ ✰

15 miles of trail that follow the Sandy River and wind throughout the park. It's easy to lose yourself in the spaciousness and ramble to your heart's content with no other thought than to see how many of the birds on the park's list (available at the office) you can identify. Wander into the old-growth forest and contemplate a summer idyll. There's a small waterfall nearby to enhance your poetic musings. Slip through the under-brush to a sun-warmed curve in the river and wriggle your toes in the sand. Even at the height of the sum-mer season, you'll be amazed at how quickly you can find seclusion.

For a different perspective of the trail system, the park allows horses on most of the pathways. There are designated equestrian unloading areas, and trailhead markers indicate those that are restricted.

Fishing and boating activities are undeniably cen-tral to the popularity of Oxbow Park and Sandy River. Most often they go hand in hand. There are very few times of the year when anglers won't find a reason to cast their lines into the broad and shallow waters. Along with its preeminent status as a steelheader's delight, the Sandy also sports healthy quantities of coho, fall and spring chinook, and summer steelhead. Check with the park office for fishing regulations on the Sandy, as they differ from those of other Oregon rivers.

Recreational boating on this section of the Sandy is limited to nonmotorized craft, thanks to the recent state and federal designations of the Wild and Scenic Sandy River. Above Oxbow Park, and dependent on flow levels, there is Class III and IV whitewater for experienced kayakers, rafters, and canoeists to enjoy. A popular run is the 6 miles between Dodge Park and Oxbow, affording exclusive views of this section of the river gorge. Downstream from Oxbow to Lewis and Clark State Park is a pleasant drift trip with gentle rip ples and refreshing pools for an occasional dip. Addi-tional river and boat-rental information is available at the park office.

If you're interested in exploring beyond the park's boundaries, Oxbow can be the starting point for a couple of scenic drives that allow you to see a lot with minimal time commitments. The shorter of the

KEY INFORMATION

ADDRESS:	Oxbow Regional Park 3010 SE Oxbow Parkway Gresham, OR 97080
OPERATED BY:	Metro
INFORMATION:	(503) 663-4708
OPEN:	All year; gates close at legal sunset and open at 6:30 a.m.
SITES:	67 total (12 for RVs)
EACH SITE HAS:	Picnic table, free-standing barbecue grill, lantern pole, shade trees
ASSIGNMENT:	First come, first served; no reserva-tions
REGISTRATION:	Daily fee collected each evening at campsite; vehicle fee at park entrance
FACILITIES:	Flush toilets, hot showers, heated-air hand dryers, and heated rest room floors; firewood for sale, group camps, playground, boat ramp, equestrian area, interpretive programs
PARKING:	At campsites (2 vehi-cles max)
FEE:	$15 plus $4 per vehi-cle entrance fee
ELEVATION:	Sea level
RESTRICTIONS:	Pets: Not permitted Fires: In fire pits only, subject to sea-sonal restrictions Alcohol: Not permit-ted Vehicles: 35-foot RV size limit, no hookups; no ATVs Other: No guns or fireworks; no gather-ing firewood

MAP

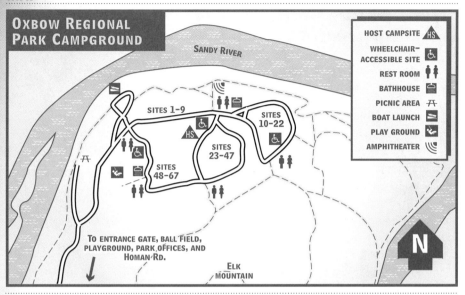

OXBOW REGIONAL PARK CAMPGROUND

SANDY RIVER

SITES 1-9

SITES 10-22

HS

SITES 23-47

SITES 48-67

TO ENTRANCE GATE, BALL FIELD, PLAYGROUND, PARK OFFICES, AND HOMAN RD.

ELK MOUNTAIN

N

HOST CAMPSITE HS
WHEELCHAIR-ACCESSIBLE SITE
REST ROOM
BATHHOUSE
PICNIC AREA
BOAT LAUNCH
PLAY GROUND
AMPHITHEATER

GETTING THERE

To reach Oxbow Park, take Exit 16, Wood Village, off I-84 in Gresham. Go south to Division Street. Turn left, and continue to Oxbow Parkway. From there, follow signs down to the park. The road winds around a bit, and there are several spots where it is easy to make a miscalculated turn. Just keep following the signs. Once you reach the park entrance, it's a sharp and curving drop down into the gorge.

two is the route along Crown Point Highway, named for the 700 foot piece of basalt that spires above the Columbia River. Crown Point Vista House, with its information center, is well worth the visit, not to mention the staggering views afforded from its lofty perch.

The second route takes you southeast on US 26 through the Sandy River lowlands, around Mount Hood, north to Hood River on SR 35, and back along I-84 to Exit 18 at Lewis and Clark State Park. This is roughly 150 miles of non-stop scenery, with the snowy peak of Mount Hood as the focal point most of the way. From Hood River back to Oxbow, the changing landscape of the Columbia River Gorge unfolds around each bend in the road.

Oxbow is a well-managed park that gives foremost consideration to the interests of its visitors. There is even a ranger on duty in the park 24 hours per day in the event of an emergency.

SILVER FALLS STATE PARK CAMPGROUND

IF YOU'RE LOOKING FOR a weekend destination where you can see it all in one place, Silver Falls State Park is the place to go. The largest state park in Oregon, the 8,700-acre Silver Falls is renowned for its hiking. The 7-mile Silver Creek Canyon Trail (also known as Trail of Ten Falls) traverses a lush forest floor covered with Oregon grape, salal, and sword ferns beneath second-growth fir, hemlock, and cedar trees.

The trail follows the north and south forks of Silver Creek, passing ten waterfalls en route. It runs behind several tall falls and along the edges of others. Bring your camera along for the South Falls, the largest, which plummets 177 feet and backs up to a tunnel through which visitors can view the cascade. If you feel like you've seen it before, you probably have, as Silver Falls is one of the most-photographed places in the state. Hiking the entire circuit can take at least three hours, so pack a picnic lunch and make an all-day excursion of it. To preserve its primitive nature, the trail is uninterrupted by picnic tables, shelters, or rest rooms.

If you want to let someone else do the walking, horse rentals are also a popular activity in this park, where you can arrange one-hour guided tours. The park includes more than 25 miles of hiking trails and 14 miles of horse trails, plus several biking paths, so there will be plenty to keep you busy (make sure to get a handy map at the park entrance). Wildlife you may spot while on the trail includes blacktail deer, black bear, and cougars, although beavers and chipmunks are more likely.

If you feel like taking a dip, there is a developed beach on the east shore of Silver Creek. There is no lifeguard on duty; rest rooms, a snack bar, and a playground are located nearby.

> *Oregon's largest state park is a destination in itself, with everything from horseback riding to waterfalls to hiking trails on its premises.*

RATINGS

Beauty: ✪ ✪ ✪
Privacy: ✪ ✪ ✪
Spaciousness: ✪ ✪ ✪
Quiet: ✪ ✪ ✪
Security: ✪ ✪ ✪ ✪
Cleanliness: ✪ ✪ ✪ ✪
Insect control: ✪ ✪ ✪

KEY INFORMATION

ADDRESS: Silver Falls
Campground
20024 Silver Falls
Highway SE
Sublimity, OR 97385

OPERATED BY: Oregon State Parks

INFORMATION: (503) 873-8681,
(800) 551-6949;
www.oregon
stateparks.org

OPEN: Mid-April through
October

SITES: 46

EACH SITE HAS: Picnic table, fire ring

ASSIGNMENT: First-come, first-
served, or by reser-
vation at (800) 452-
5687 or www.reserve
america.com ($6 fee)

REGISTRATION: At park entrance

FACILITIES: Flush toilets, hot
showers

PARKING: At campsites and at
park entrance

FEE: $12, $7 per additional vehicle

ELEVATION: 250 feet

RESTRICTIONS: Pets: On leash only
(dogs are not
allowed on the Trail
of Ten Falls)
Fires: In fire rings
only
Alcohol: At camp-
sites only
Vehicles: One per
site
Other: 14-day stay
limit

Silver Falls State Park took its name from the former town of Silver Falls City, population 200, which
stood where the South Falls parking lot now lies. (It
officially became a park in the early 1930s.) Evidence
of the town's main source of income—logging—remains
in some of the park's large cedar stumps—notches from
springboards the loggers wedged into the trees' trunks
to cut them. At the historic South Falls lodge, you can
enjoy a post-hike latté and take a glimpse back into
history through the collection of old logging photos
and antique tools. The lodge, originally designed as a
restaurant, was constructed by the Civilian Conservation Corps and Works Project Administration in the
1930s, closed in the late 1950s, and restored pursuant
to its placement on the National Register of Historic
Places in 1983. All of the more than 100 pieces of fur-
niture in the lodge was crafted from two myrtlewood
logs 5 feet in diameter and 40 feet long.

The nearby town of Silverton is home to the Silverton Historical Museum, in a 1908 home, which
offers more photographs and artifacts from the area's
farming and logging history. Visit in July to catch the
annual Al Faussett Days festival, commemorating Faussett's 1928 plunge over South Falls in a canvas canoe.
Present-day Faussett family members converge at the
falls along with hundreds of visitors who are treated to
a newsreel of the actual event.

While many campgrounds are more of jumping-
off points for nearby attractions, Silver Falls is one
area that neatly encompasses all activities in its boundaries. Cabins are also available for rent, and there are
several group-camping sites as well. Although the park
does tend to get a little crowded because it's so popular—and long has been, even decades before the first
land was deeded to the state for a park—it's also quite
easy to lose the crowds because of its sheer size.

Despite the area's name, no one has struck it rich
mining silver, gold, or any other ore here, but the
park's natural wonders are a perfect example of our
most precious commodities.

MAP

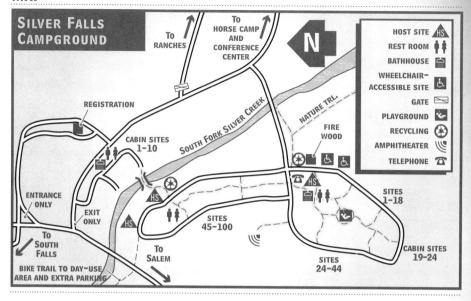

GETTING THERE

From Salem, drive east on OR 22 for 5 miles to OR 214. Turn left and drive 15 miles to the park entrance.

SUMMIT LAKE CAMPGROUND

> *Summit Lake is small and simple but with generously sized walk-in sites—all with lake views.*

THE NAME'S A BIT MISLEADING, as there is no sense of having reached the top of something when you get to Summit Lake. But once you're here, you'll be on top of the world and so proud of yourself for having found this wonderfully simple yet delightful spot far from the Timothy Lake crowds.

Summit Lake is on the order of Rujada (see page 116)—a great place to visit when you don't have a lot of time and don't want a heavy agenda. Unlike Rujada, it's underdeveloped and primitive, with mostly walk-in sites either anchored by the shoreline or on a slight inland incline with a lake view.

Access to Summit Lake is almost too easy, which is what makes the lack of crowds so surprising. It could be that the magnetic draw of Timothy Lake, with its eye-popping views of Mount Hood, is all it takes to divert impressionable campers. It also could be that those who value a sublime place like Summit Lake aren't about to share it with others. The most plausible theory of all is that most people are driving way too fast on the Oregon Skyline Road (FS 42 in Forest Service) to see the very small, dark-brown wooden sign engulfed in roadside foliage pointing the way to Summit Lake down FS 141.

Whatever the reasons, Summit Lake shows up on detailed topographic maps as the tiniest blue slash alongside the Skyline Road, and those of us who have discovered its charms hope the campground retains its rustic, untrammeled character.

Here's a simple lesson in how to enjoy Summit Lake: Drive the mile of decent gravel off the Skyline Road down FS 141, park the car in the group-parking area, take a short walk along one of the camp trails, pick the spot of your choice (may not have as many choices on the weekend), and then unload the car. Total time from turning off Skyline Road: 20 minutes.

RATINGS

Beauty: ✪ ✪ ✪ ✪
Privacy: ✪ ✪ ✪ ✪
Spaciousness: ✪ ✪ ✪ ✪ ✪
Quiet: ✪ ✪ ✪ ✪ ✪
Security: ✪ ✪ ✪ ✪ ✪
Cleanliness: ✪ ✪ ✪ ✪ ✪
Insect control: ✪ ✪ ✪

Summit Lake will appear on your left as you drive along FS 141, so enjoy the preview. Campsites 1 and 2 are the only drive-in sites, but I don't consider them the best sites because they have very little privacy and are opposite the parking area for the walk-in sites. I imagine it gets noisy and busy with engines starting, doors slamming (there should be a camp rule against this), and gear being transported.

Go for sites 4 and 5 if you can. These are the farthest from the parking area so toting a lot of stuff can be a bit of a drag, and you have to pass the other campsites getting there. (Keep to the trail; cutting through other campsites is a major camping faux pas.) Sites 4 and 5 offer the best vantage for enjoying lake views and those early morning sunrises. Site 3 isn't all bad, but it sits fairly near the parking area. Sites 7 and 8 sit back from the lake but are bounded on all sides by the trails that lead through the campground, perhaps an annoying element when children are chasing each other through the underbrush oblivious to your tent nearby. Site 6 sits alone up a small grade and has the best overview of the lake and the other campsites.

In general, the sites are spacious with a smattering of foliage in between to soften the views, but I would not describe the underbrush as lush or the campsites as shrouded. A tent positioned in the right way can do a lot to act as a curtain. What these sites lack in privacy, however, they make up for by being spaced well apart. Each has the basic amenities—picnic table, grill—and they share a modern vault toilet near the parking area. Garbage services are a notable plus.

The Oregon Skyline Road, which passes by Summit Lake, cuts a mid-elevation swath between the dense Mount Hood National Forest on its western flank and the rolling ridges of the Warm Springs Indian Reservation to the east. It ultimately meets up with FS 46, which continues northward as Clackamas River Road and becomes Breitenbush Road to the south before its junction with OR 22 at Detroit.

Recreational opportunities abound, with two scenic byways to explore, the Wild and Scenic Clackamas River to admire, trout-stocked lakes to tackle, and

KEY INFORMATION

ADDRESS: Summit Lake Campground c/o Zigzag Ranger District 65000 East US 26 Welches, OR 97067

OPERATED BY: Thousand Trails for Mount Hood National Forest

INFORMATION: (503) 622-7674

OPEN: Late May through September

SITES: 2 drive-in sites; 6 walk-in sites

EACH SITE HAS: Picnic table, fire grill

ASSIGNMENT: First come, first served; no reservations

REGISTRATION: Self-registration on site

FACILITIES: Vault toilets, piped water, garbage service

PARKING: In parking area

FEE: $10

ELEVATION: 4,200 feet

RESTRICTIONS: Pets: On leash only
Fires: In fire pits only
Alcohol: Permitted
Vehicles: 16-foot RV size limit, no hookups
Other: 14-day limit on stay; nonmotorized boats only on lake

MAP

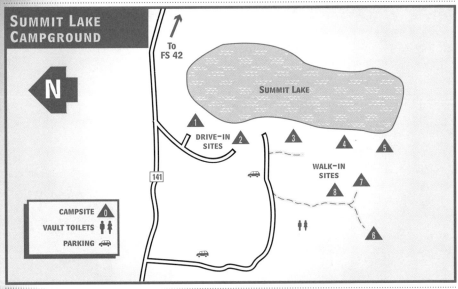

SUMMIT LAKE
CAMPGROUND

N

To
FS 42

SUMMIT LAKE

1

DRIVE-IN
SITES 2

3

4

5

141

WALK-IN
SITES

7

8

6

CAMPSITE 0
VAULT TOILETS
PARKING

GETTING THERE

From the intersection of US
26 and OR 35 on the south
side of Mount Hood (just
past Government Camp),
drive east on US 26 for 15
miles to FS 42 (also known
as Skyline Road). Drive for
12 gravel miles to FS 141.
The sign is nearly hidden by
vegetation, so watch your
mileage. Turn right onto FS
141 and follow it for about a
mile. Summit Lake will be
on your left.

endless mountain ridges to wander. Bring a good map,
a set of binoculars, a comfortable pair of boots, and
however much time you can spare. You may not
accomplish everything on this trip, but it's not too far
to come back soon.

CENTRAL **CASCADES**
AND ENVIRONS

FRISSELL CROSSING CAMPGROUND

WHEN YOU DRIVE ALONG the Aufderheide Memorial Drive (named for a former Willamette National Forest supervisor) on your way to Frissell Crossing, try not to think about what I did: lions, and tigers, and bears . . . and flying monkeys, and wicked witches. Oh, my!

I happened to be alone. I didn't stop with *The Wizard of Oz*, either. I was Little Red Riding Hood eluding the Big Bad Wolf; I was Gretel without Hansel; I was Scout from *To Kill A Mockingbird* coming home from the Halloween party in her ham costume.

It's easy to let your imagination run wild as you wind along the Aufderheide, whether you approach it from the South Fork McKenzie River side on the north at Blue River or from the North Fork Middle Fork Willamette on the south at Westfir. Some of you will read that sentence at least twice, puzzling over the route. The road, 65 miles long, follows in modern style the pioneering wagon route established by miners and loggers in the late 1800s. As it rises and falls through dense old-growth forest and passes over a low-elevation saddle between the two river drainages, a rich mosaic of historical, geological, and cultural significance is revealed. It would be easy to fill a week absorbing it all between backcountry exploration and roadside edification.

If you don't have that kind of time but still want to get the most out of what the Aufderheide has to offer, take the auto tape tour. The Forest Service provides free-of-charge either a cassette or CD that you can pick up and drop off at various locations on both the north and south entry points to the drive. To my mind, this is a far better idea than having your nose buried in a guidebook (excluding this volume, of course). For one thing, it's kind of dangerous to read and drive at the same time. Second, you can't always prepare in

> *The drive getting to Frissell is as much a part of the adventure as the camping experience itself.*

RATINGS

Beauty: ✿ ✿ ✿ ✿ ✿
Privacy: ✿ ✿ ✿
Spaciousness: ✿ ✿ ✿ ✿ ✿
Quiet: ✿ ✿ ✿ ✿ ✿
Security: ✿ ✿
Cleanliness: ✿ ✿ ✿
Insect control: ✿ ✿

ADDRESS: Frissell Crossing
Campground
c/o McKenzie River
Ranger District
57600 McKenzie
Highway
McKenzie Bridge,
OR 97413

OPERATED BY: HooDoo Recreation
Services for
Willamette National
Forest

INFORMATION: (541) 822-3799 or
(541) 822-3381
(ranger district)

OPEN: May through
September

SITES: 12

EACH SITE HAS: Picnic table, fire grill

ASSIGNMENT: First come, first
served; no reserva-
tions

REGISTRATION: Self-registration on
site

FACILITIES: Vault toilets, hand-
pumped water

PARKING: At campsites

FEE: $10 per night; $5 per
additional vehicle

ELEVATION: 2,600 feet

RESTRICTIONS: Pets: On leash only
Fires: In fire pits
only
Alcohol: Permitted
Vehicles: RVs up to
36 feet (turnaround
space is limited); no
hookups
Other: 14-day stay
limit

advance if your camping tendencies are as sponta-
neous as mine. So, read my book first, refer to it when
you've stopped at a viewpoint, but keep the tape running while you're driving. I hope this tape tour signals
a trend for other agencies, which may elect to manage
their scenic byways in a similar fashion. I've always
thought similar narration would be a great addition to
train travel, too, but that's a different conversation.

Frissell Crossing Campground sits at about the
one-third mark on the Aufderheide—from its northern
terminus—along the South Fork McKenzie River,
which has made a quick descent from its source in the
Mink Lake Basin. Although you'll pass several other
campgrounds along the route, Frissell Crossing has one
thing most others don't: piped water. The camping
sites are situated well away from the main road, too,
which I always prefer.

Minimally developed sites are spread around an
open meadow, retaining in ambience the true essence
of the Aufderheide and the primarily roadless wilderness land surrounding the campground. A high canopy
of old growth Douglas fir further lends to the sense of
space at Frissell Crossing, while generous low-growing
vegetation creates a gentle buffer between campsites
and adds just the right measure of privacy without
claustrophobia. The McKenzie passes through grassy,
rhododendron-shrouded banks on the campground's
southern border.

With only 12 sites, it's unlikely you'll ever feel
crowded, but sites 6 and 7 on the eastern edge of the
campground loop are the most removed from the main
activity area. During the week, it's not unlikely that you
would have the place to yourself. When I visited in
mid-August, only three spaces were taken. Certainly no
guarantee, but the Aufderheide, one of the first 50
drives in the country to receive federal scenic byway
designation in 1988, is not among the more heavily
traveled routes in Oregon.

Use Frissell Crossing as a base camp for hiking for-
ays into a multitude of wilderness areas. Due east is the
south-central sector of the Three Sisters Wilderness,
which laps over into the western Cascades and is far
less traveled than its northern counterpart. This region

MAP

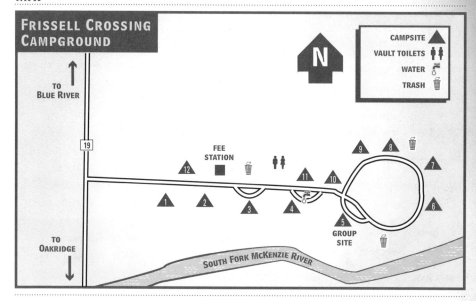

FRISSELL CROSSING CAMPGROUND

TO
BLUE RIVER

19

FEE
STATION

TO
OAKRIDGE

SOUTH FORK MCKENZIE RIVER

N

CAMPSITE ▲
VAULT TOILETS 🚻
WATER
TRASH 🗑

12

1 2 3 4 5

11 10

9 8

7

6

GROUP
SITE

of the wilderness is home to a stunning cluster of alpine lakes and the headwaters of the South Fork McKenzie. On Frissell's north side is the French Pete Creek area, the inclusion of which into Three Sisters Wilderness in 1978 preserved some of the most accessible examples of ancient low-elevation old growth. A short drive south of Frissell is the trailhead for access into the northern portion of the Waldo Lake Wilderness.

Driving the Aufderheide requires that you check the gas gauge first. There are absolutely no services along the route, and side trips can eat up your fuel supply. Bring plenty of food rations, too. You just never know where the Willamette's version of the Yellow Brick Road may lead.

Ruby hiking boots, anyone?

GETTING THERE

From Blue River, take OR 126 4 miles east to FS 19 (Aufderheide Memorial Drive). Turn right and follow the Aufderheide for 21.5 miles to Frissell Crossing Campground. The campground entrance is on the left. From Westfir, drive north on FS 19 for just about 43 miles to the campground on the right.

LOWER PALISADES CAMPGROUND

> *You can practically fly-fish from your campsite in this secluded spot along the Wild and Scenic Crooked River.*

AT FIRST GLANCE, YOU probably wouldn't expect Lower Palisades to qualify for inclusion in this book. It's a string of dusty, sparsely vegetated, one-step-up-from-dispersed-camping sites abutting a rock wall on one of the narrowest necks of the upper Crooked River.

But let's suppose that you made a bet with your camping buddies that you would point to any camping spot on the state overview map accompanying this book. And let's further suppose that you are a fly-fishing fanatic (licensees and identification will be checked at the campground entrance). And finally let's suppose that you refuse to violate the basic tenets of this book regarding campground aesthetics.

All these elements considered, you cannot improve on Lower Palisades as the best camping choice of the numerous Bureau of Land Management sites along this Wild and Scenic stretch of the Crooked River. I put the remainder (seven others) to the weekday and weekend test. Except for Lower Palisades, they all failed miserably. Sorry, BLM.

The main reason for their exclusion here: RVs. Scads of them. Fleets of them. None smaller than a railroad car (or so it seemed). Circled like Conestoga wagons, presumably to protect themselves against the warlike tent campers. Lined up like Roman phalanxes approaching the walled city. Parked at crazy angles to take optimum advantage of a view only they could enjoy. I think that covers it.

A second reason for Lower Palisades inclusion is the campground's proximity to the main road. Although these BLM campgrounds fall within the Crooked River Backcountry Scenic Byway corridor, I can't recommend camping where you can see (or hear, for that matter) cars going by on their scenic way. Lower Palisades is the only one of the eight

RATINGS

Beauty: ☆ ☆ ☆ ☆
Privacy: ☆ ☆ ☆
Spaciousness: ☆ ☆ ☆
Quiet: ☆ ☆ ☆ ☆
Security: ☆ ☆
Cleanliness: ☆ ☆
Insect control: ☆ ☆ ☆

campgrounds that offers some relief on this front. It's tucked at the bottom of a small gorge where the river has carved a sharp bend. From the road above, the Lower Palisades Campground is invisible. The only indication that a campground exists here is the signboard at its entrance. The canyon winds lift the sounds of civilization up, and any road noise that might be tempted downwards will bounce off the sheer basalt walls on the opposite side of the river or be drowned out by the swift-flowing water.

Primitively developed and well-spaced, all campsites at Lower Palisades have the roadside slope of the canyon wall at their backs and the river at their feet. Parking spaces are designed as pull-throughs with tent sites on the riverside. Although the pull-throughs are usually provided for the turnaround ease of RVs, the turning radius at Lower Palisades is quite tight even for a normal car. Given this logistical limitation, most RVs that maneuver down here at all find themselves regretting not having stopped at Castle Rock, Stillwater, or Lone Pine or pressed on to Chimney Rock or Big Bend. Give them a hand if they are in danger of backing into the river and send them on their way.

Of the campsites, only sites 9, 10, and 13 are on the non-river side of the access road but the view across the road to the river is unobstructed. These may not be the best spots but will do if everything else is taken. Sites 11 and 12 could be the premium spaces, as they sit most removed from the main activity areas of the campground at the north end and just above the river, with views in both directions and out of the shadow of the palisade. Site 12 shares its parking loop with Site 13, a minor consideration.

If you've come for the fishing, be aware that the Crooked River has gained a distinctive following. At the height of the season, the river is chock full not only of plump rainbow trout, but also a bevy of fly-fishing purists who look as though they walked right out of an Orvis catalogue or a Robert Redford movie.

Beyond the allure (no pun intended) of fly-fishing, the Crooked River offers an opportunity to walk on the wild side and learn about the geology, flora, and

KEY INFORMATION

ADDRESS:	Lower Palisades Campground c/o Prineville District Office 3050 NE Third Street Prineville, OR 97754
OPERATED BY:	Bureau of Land Management
INFORMATION:	(541) 416-6700
OPEN:	Year-round
SITES:	15
EACH SITE HAS:	Picnic table, fire gril; some shade trees
ASSIGNMENT:	First come, first served; no reservations
REGISTRATION:	Self-registration on site
FACILITIES:	Vault toilets (wheelchair accessible), piped water, garbage service, one group site, picnic area
PARKING:	At campsites
FEE:	$8, $2 per additional vehicle
ELEVATION:	2,900 feet
RESTRICTIONS:	**Pets:** On leash only **Fires:** In fire pits only **Alcohol:** Permitted **Vehicles:** Large trailers not recommended **Other:** 14-day stay limit

MAP

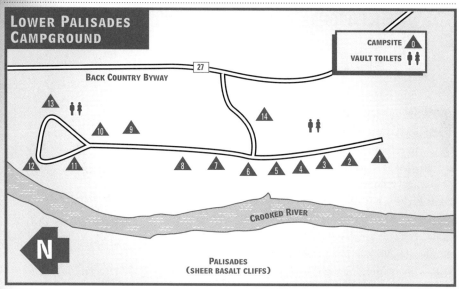

LOWER PALISADES CAMPGROUND

CAMPSITE
VAULT TOILETS

BACK COUNTRY BYWAY

27

13

10   9

14

12   11

8   7   6   5   4   3   2   1

CROOKED RIVER

N

PALISADES
(SHEER BASALT CLIFFS)

GETTING THERE

From Prineville, turn south on SR 27 and follow it for 15.3 paved miles to the campground. The road is also known as the Crooked River Backcountry Scenic Byway.

fauna of the rim country that rises above. From the Chimney Rock campground next door to Lower Palisades, the Rim Tail quickly gets you up on the high desert floor with a reasonable hike under 2 miles (one way) to Chimney Rock. Scenic viewpoints appear along the way, and it is not uncommon to observe wildlife. The BLM has put together an exhaustive three-page list of the plantlife along the trail, which is great if you know what you're looking at. Next comes a photographic guide? Nevertheless, it's astonishing to see the variety of vegetation that survives in the harsh environs of Oregon's rimrock lands.

The remaining scenic-byway route continues on past Bowman Dam and connects with US 20 over an unforgiving gravel washboard. This is better traveled via mountain bike, in my mind. An alternative auto route leads back into Prineville and down towards Prineville Reservoir State Park.

MALLARD MARSH CAMPGROUND

FOR REASONS UNKNOWN BUT perfectly acceptable to me, Mallard Marsh gets short shrift in
much of the literature about the Central Oregon
Cascade Lakes region. Perhaps because the campground name doesn't reflect its location on Hosmer
Lake? Perhaps because the term marsh implies a
soggy, bug-infested ordeal? Perhaps because Western-
ers just can't accept the idea of Atlantic salmon being
introduced into their pristine waters? Or maybe just
because there are so many camping options in this
Mecca for outdoor adventure?

Whatever the reason, I am going to raise aware-
ness by saying that Mallard Marsh is likely one of the
prettiest campground settings you'll find listed in this
book. It has lots of competition from countless other
lakes in the region, too, but for one reason or another,
none measure up to the outstanding tent camping features of Mallard Marsh. I know that's saying a lot, but
it's hard to deny the exquisite combination of Hosmer
Lake's deepest blue waters, azure skies, brilliant green
marsh grasses, and colorful waterfowl, topped off with
a snowstreaked volcano cone as the backdrop. It simply doesn't get much more picturesque!

The campground itself maintains a very natural
countenance to further add to its charm. Driving in
past the busy boat launch, you can pick your spot as
you pass between the sites, roughly half on the lakeside and the others discreetly tucked on little knolls
and in slight depressions. All of the sites are situated
under tall stands of lodgepole pine, Douglas fir and
mountain hemlock, with heavy undergrowth of salal,
laurel, and huckleberry providing effective natural
screening for privacy. The sites along the lake tend to
be a bit more open and enjoy the morning sun's rays
earlier. The sites set back receive filtered sunlight all
day long and probably are less mosquito-prone.

> *Deep blue waters,
> azure skies, brilliant
> green marshes and a
> snowcapped volcano
> comprise the scene at
> Mallard Marsh—one of
> the prettiest camp-
> ground settings in this
> book.*

RATINGS

Beauty: ✿ ✿ ✿ ✿ ✿
Privacy: ✿ ✿ ✿ ✿ ✿
Spaciousness: ✿ ✿ ✿ ✿ ✿
Quiet: ✿ ✿ ✿ ✿ ✿
Security: ✿ ✿ ✿ ✿
Cleanliness: ✿ ✿ ✿ ✿ ✿
Insect control: ✿ ✿

ADDRESS: Mallard Marsh
Campground
c/o Bend/Fort Rock
Ranger District
1230 NE Third
Street, Suite A-262
Bend, OR 97701

OPERATED BY: High Lakes Contractors for Deschutes
National Forest

INFORMATION: (541) 383-4000

OPEN: May to late September

SITES: 23

EACH SITE HAS: Picnic table, fire pit

ASSIGNMENT: First come, first
served; no reservations

REGISTRATION: Self-registration on
site

FACILITIES: Vault toilets, no
piped water, boat
launch nearby

PARKING: At campsites

FEE: $5

ELEVATION: 5,000 feet

RESTRICTIONS: Pets: On leash only
Fires: In fire pits
only
Alcohol: Permitted
Vehicles: 22-feet RV
size limit, no
hookups
Other: Electric boat
motors only

In general, the spaciousness of the sites and the generous greenbelts between them lend a delightfully uncrowded feel to the camping experience at Mallard Marsh, even at the height of a busy summer week. When I pulled into a lakeside drive-through site and walked down to check out the general lay of the land, I could barely see my car not more than ten yards away!

In this setting, Hosmer Lake is a sport fisherman's dream, but it's one that comes with a few regulations. In order to challenge the wily Atlantic salmon and brown trout that ply the lake's waters, only fly-fishing with barbless hooks is allowed. Nonmotorized boats are the approved mode of travel.

While sailboaters and windsurfers head for Elk Lake when the wind is up, Hosmer is ideal for muscle-powered water travel (i.e. kayaks and canoes) that better suit the quiet ambience of the place anyway. Encompassing only 160 acres, Hosmer makes it easy to spend a lazy afternoon exploring the bordering wetlands and taking in a little birdwatching. Don't forget the binoculars.

The Cascade Lakes region is home to many high-country rambles if the trail calls you out of your lakeside comfort. From the Cascade Lakes Highway, you can satisfy your explorer's urge with trailheads in all directions. Quite possibly, you'll be following along routes established by the early trappers and adventurers who left their indelible historical mark on the region. You could easily spend a full week just on the trails of the Three Sisters Wilderness (due west of Hosmer Lake), discovering one alpine lake gem after another and getting your boots dusty on a section of the Pacific Crest Trail in one of its easiest wilderness access points. From some of the higher vantage points, you can practically watch the weather patterns changing overhead as this is a meeting point for air currents where rapid climatic transition occurs.

Like many of the ancient landmarks that give Oregon its remarkable diversity, the Cascade Lakes region was defined geologically by cataclysmic events that occurred millions of years ago. Unlike many other parts of Oregon, the contours of the landscape, the composition of the soils, and the nature of the

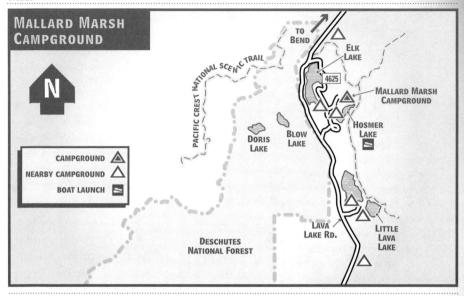

MALLARD MARSH
CAMPGROUND

N

TO BEND

ELK LAKE

4625

MALLARD MARSH
CAMPGROUND

PACIFIC CREST NATIONAL SCENIC TRAIL

HOSMER
LAKE

DORIS
LAKE

BLOW
LAKE

CAMPGROUND

NEARBY CAMPGROUND

BOAT LAUNCH

LAVA
LAKE RD.

DESCHUTES
NATIONAL FOREST

LITTLE
LAVA
LAKE

vegetation make it possible to view many of Central Oregon's treasures up close. A good place to start is the Lava Lands Visitor Center or High Desert Museum in Bend. Spend an afternoon there and you'll leave much better prepared for understanding the wonders that await.

One word of warning if you intend to do some daytripping. The closest services to Mallard Marsh are either in Bend or LaPine, and it is easy to lose track of time and distance out here. Make sure you've got a full gas tank.

GETTING THERE

From Bend, follow signs for the Cascade Lakes Highway (FS 46) west around the north side of Mount Bachelor for 35.5 miles. At FS 4625, turn left and drive 1.3 miles to the campground, which will be on your left. You'll bypass Elk Lake on your way to Mallard Marsh. If heading north on the Cascade Lakes Highway, take FS 4625 to the right about 4 miles beyond the Lava Lake Road. At the Y, turn right down the gravel road; turn left just before the boat launch area and you're there.

RIVERSIDE CAMPGROUND

> *One of many campgrounds near the fisherman's paradise that is the Metolius River.*

AH, THE MAGICAL AND mysterious Metolius. Welling up clear and bright from a tiny underground spring at the base of Black Butte and providing one of the finest trout habitats around (catch-and-release fly-fishing only) before emptying into the Deschutes River.

There are varying theories about the exact origins of this headwater phenomenon, but the prevailing one seems to be that ancient earth movements blocked the original Metolius and forced it to find an alternate route. It took a while, but it eventually found an outlet at the base of Black Butte. Today, it bubbles and burbles at a rate of 50,000 gallons per minute (right before your very eyes!) to create one of the coldest and clearest rivers in Oregon.

That's why trout like it so much. However, there was a time when salmon sought its cooling waters, too. The word Metolius derives from mytolyas, a term that showed up in a nineteenth-century Pacific Railroad survey report. The reference is to a variety of salmon that is no longer found in the river. Fishermen, on the other hand, will be in plentiful supply if you come to the Metolius at the height of the fly-fishing season. The number of campgrounds on or near the Metolius is staggering, and they are there primarily to serve the abundance of anglers. In addition to Riverside, campers can choose from Camp Sherman, Allingham, Smiling River, Pine Rest, Gorge, Allen Springs, Pioneer Ford, and Lower Bridge.

Riverside is notable in that it has only walk-in sites, which are spacious, grassy, and well-situated under stands of majestic old ponderosa pine. Parking spaces are numbered to correspond with campsites, each within a reasonable distance of the other, but the best sites (those closest to the river) will suddenly seem a long way away if you've got a lot of heavy,

RATINGS

Beauty: ✪ ✪ ✪ ✪
Privacy: ✪ ✪ ✪
Spaciousness: ✪ ✪ ✪ ✪
Quiet: ✪ ✪ ✪ ✪
Security: ✪ ✪ ✪
Cleanliness: ✪ ✪ ✪
Insect control: ✪ ✪ ✪ ✪

cumbersome gear. A small wheelbarrow would be quite useful. (Maybe someone should write to the Sisters Ranger District).

This area of central Oregon is characterized by warm—even hot—and dry summers and cold, snowy winters. Upland areas have been known to receive as much as 20 feet of snow, and many trails will be blocked well into May. The terrain is laid with a volcanic base, out of which spills a dazzling collage of crystalline streams, creeks, and rivers. Ancient lava flows, dormant and deteriorated craters, sparkling inlays of obsidian, rugged basalt cliffs, flat-topped mesas and buttes, and numerous lakes dot the landscape.

Dominating the landscape in various stages of geologic splendor are the snowcapped peaks to the west. In order from north to south, they are: Mount Jefferson, Mount Washington, North Sister, Middle Sister, South Sister, and last but not least, despite its forlorn name, Broken Top.

Hiking is one of the best ways to fully appreciate the diversity of this region. There are actually four distinct geographic zones all observable at once: the high-alpine slopes of the volcanoes, with meadows of wildflowers and crumbling lava rock; subalpine forests of ponderosa pine and mountain hemlock nourished by cascading streams and glacial lakes; steep-walled canyons that protect the last of the old-growth fir; and arid pockets of lodgepole pine interspersed with bear grass.

Besides foot travel, other ways to take in the scenery are by horseback and mountain bike. Retrace the routes of such early-day explorers as Lewis and Clark, Kit Carson, and John Fremont on the Metolius-Windigo Trail. Outfitters in Sisters can help you with any hoofed mode of travel.

For cyclists, a 30-mile loop trip along the crest of Green Ridge provides panoramic views of the Cascades. It's a climb of 1,700 feet to the top, and it would be advisable to have a map of the route handy as you ride. This is good advice for anyone who plans to explore places not in the immediate vicinity of FS 14 along the Metolius. There is a crazy network of spur

KEY INFORMATION

ADDRESS:	Riverside Campground c/o Sisters Ranger District P.O. Box 249 Sisters, OR 97759
OPERATED BY:	Concessionaire for Deschutes National Forest
INFORMATION:	(541) 549-2111
OPEN:	Mid-April to mid-October
SITES:	16
EACH SITE HAS:	Picnic table, fire grill; some shade trees
ASSIGNMENT:	First come, first served; no reservation
REGISTRATION:	Self-registration on site
FACILITIES:	Vault toilets, hand-pumped water
PARKING:	At access road, roughly 200–400 yards from campground
FEE:	$10, $5 per additional vehicle
ELEVATION:	3,000 feet
RESTRICTIONS:	**Pets:** On leash only **Fires:** In fire pits only **Alcohol:** Permitted **Vehicles:** 21-foot RV size limit, no hookups **Other:** 14-day stay limit

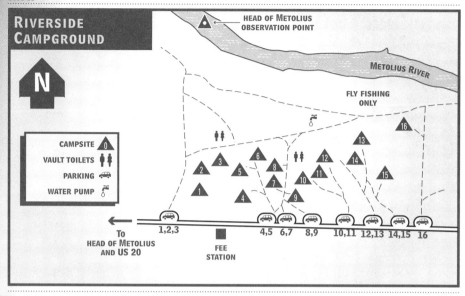

RIVERSIDE CAMPGROUND

HEAD OF METOLIUS
OBSERVATION POINT

METOLIUS RIVER

FLY FISHING
ONLY

N

CAMPSITE
VAULT TOILETS
PARKING
WATER PUMP

To
HEAD OF METOLIUS
AND US 20

1,2,3

FEE
STATION

4,5 6,7 8,9 10,11 12,13 14,15 16

GETTING THERE

Take SR 126/US 20 (Santiam Highway) north of Sisters to its intersection with FS 14 (Camp Sherman Road). Turn right, and follow FS 14 around the base of Black Butte to FS 900. The camp is less than a mile north on this road. There are some services in Camp Sherman.

roads that can easily lead you astray if you don't know your way around.

I can't in good faith recommend the Metolius as a boating choice, although it is set up delightfully for water-based recreation. Be aware that the opposite side of the Metolius at Riverside is private land and should be respected as such. Farther downstream, the Warm Springs Tribe has jurisdiction over a contentious stretch of the river. If you're looking for a float, I suggest somewhere else or you may be looking at a fight! Check with the Sisters Ranger Station for the latest in this prickly situation and alternate options.

Highlights of a stay at Riverside Campground include short walks to Metolius Spring and Jack Creek Spring, the Metolius River Canyon near Camp Sherman, and the Wizard Falls Fish Hatchery (a surprisingly beautiful setting, unlike most hatcheries).

THREE CREEK AND DRIFTWOOD CAMPGROUNDS

IF ONE COULD CHOOSE a campsite via aerial surveillance and parachute in, Three Creek and Driftwood would top my list. I would set my sights on site 17 at Driftwood and "Geronimoooo!" Beam me up in a week, Scotty . . .

How is it that the worst 2 miles of any given forest road are the last?! Darned if I didn't feel as though there was a *Candid Camera* photographer lurking in the bushes as I approached Three Creek Lake. Smoothly making great time on the loooong grade up out of Sisters, I was patting myself on the back for all the extra time I would have to explore the Metolius River later that day. I distinctly remember saying to myself, "This road is a piece of cake! What a treat!"

Wham! Whoa! Washboard. Washout. Whatever. What a nightmare! I limped along over the last 2 miles, even considered bailing on this one despite the high recommendation. Now that I think about it, that recommendation came third- or fourth-hand by someone who had heard from somebody who told so-and-so. You know how rumors get started.

I'm glad I persevered, however, because Three Creek Lake is a spectacularly beautiful, high-altitude gem that offers a quality tent-camping experience.

And since I made it here, I'm giving you a choice of two campgrounds. Driftwood is the nearer to Sisters by about a mile (making it a winner in my mind) and Three Creek is at road's end. Driftwood sprawls around the north shore of Three Creek Lake with 17 sites and Three Creek is tucked in on the south side with a cozy 10. Both campgrounds charge the same fee ($12), both are at the same elevation (6,600 feet), and both are quite rustic, without piped water but with garbage service through HooDoo Recreation Service.

Driftwood is accessed off the main road, FS 16, by a short spur to the right. Go for one of the campsites

> *The last 2 miles will challenge your driving skills—and patience—but your reward is a high-altitude tent camper's paradise.*

RATINGS

Beauty: ✿ ✿ ✿ ✿ ✿
Privacy: ✿ ✿ ✿ (Three Creek)
　　　　✿ ✿ ✿ ✿ (Driftwood)
Spaciousness: ✿ ✿ ✿ ✿
Quiet: ✿ ✿ ✿ ✿ ✿
Security: ✿ ✿ ✿ ✿
Cleanliness: ✿ ✿ ✿ ✿ ✿
Insect Control: ✿ ✿ ✿

KEY INFORMATION

ADDRESS:	Three Creeks Lake Campground c/o Sisters Ranger District P.O. Box 249 Sisters, OR 97759
OPERATED BY:	HooDoo Recreation Service for Deschutes National Forest
INFORMATION:	(541) 549-7700
OPEN:	Late May to mid-October, depending on snow level
SITES:	10
EACH SITE HAS:	Picnic table, fire grill; some shade trees
ASSIGNMENT:	First come, first serve; no reservations
REGISTRATION:	Self-registration on site
FACILITIES:	Vault toilets, no piped water, garbage service
PARKING:	At campsites
FEE:	$12, $6 per additional vehicle
ELEVATION:	6,600 feet
RESTRICTIONS:	**Pets:** On leash only **Fires:** In fire pits only **Alcohol:** Permitted **Vehicles:** 20-foot RV size limit, no hookups **Other:** 14-day stay limit, nonmotorized boats only

around the farthest perimeter of the lake and you will be ensconced in what feels like your own private reserve, with lots of vegetation and tree cover all around. The drill for these sites is to park your car up above and pack your gear down to the tent site, situated well back from the lake's edge. In fact, most of the sites have their parking space well away from the actual tent-pitching and campfire area. I like this design as it maintains the immediate surroundings outside your tent in a very natural state.

Sites along the spur road closer to the main road are more open, trading heavy vegetation for more of a beachy feel. I saw fishermen on the shore in front of their campsite relaxing in camp chairs with fishing lines extended out into the lake. Maybe not the most die-hard anglers, but they were getting their money's worth out of the campsite!

At Three Creek Campground, the sites are arranged on either side of the small loop road. Privacy is not as characteristic here, although all sites share a general feeling of being off the beaten path (well-beaten, as a matter of fact). There are a few sites closer to the lake that have the appearance of constant RV wear and tear. Avoid these and choose one of the sites perched on the hillside overlooking the lake.

Most people come to Three Creek Lake for the fishing. But with the massive presence of Tam McArthur Rim, which blocks the view of the craggy peaks in the Three Sisters Wilderness just beyond, you know you could be on the brink of a classic alpine adventure. Three Sisters Wilderness is one of the most heavily traveled areas of Central Oregon. It's also one of the larger tracts at 285,202 acres, and because access points from the north tend to be limited to a few spur roads off FS 16, this section of Three Sisters can be surprisingly lonely.

The trailhead for Tam McArthur leaves from Three Creek Lake adjacent to Driftwood Campground, and since you can see where you're headed, the only way out is up. Once you've reached the top of the rim, however, the trail flattens out. The best views of the Three Sisters cluster (North, Middle, and South Sister, as well as Broken Top Mountains) are a

MAP

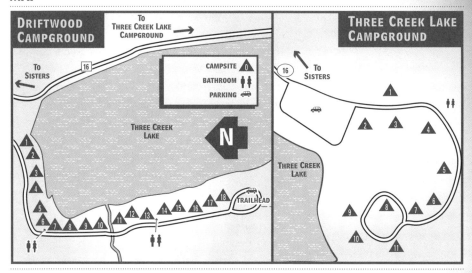

little farther along the trail. Numerous link trails will take you to an assortment of alpine lakes and more views of the heart of the Cascades.

Except for the last couple miles of FS 16, the drive up to Driftwood and Three Creek is not particularly eventful or memorable. The valley floor falls away quickly, but what views can be had are mostly in the rearview mirror or filtered through the lodgepole and ponderosa pines that line this highway. Sit back, enjoy the open road in front of you and hold onto your teeth for the last 2 miles. Then, once you've arrived, have your fill of lake fishing, mountainous hiking, and breathtaking vistas.

Okay, Scotty, I'm ready!

GETTING THERE

From US 20 in Sisters, turn south on FS 16 and drive for 17 miles up, up, up to the campground. The last 2 miles are torturously washboarded, so go slow, slow, slow (unlike everyone else).

TRAIL BRIDGE CAMPGROUND

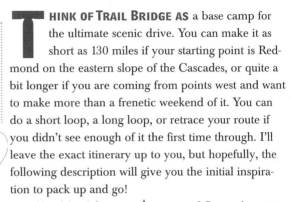

> *Looking for a scenic drive with a convenient campground along the way? A trip to Oregon can't be considered complete until you have driven the McKenzie River Loop.*

THINK OF **T**RAIL **B**RIDGE **AS** a base camp for the ultimate scenic drive. You can make it as short as 130 miles if your starting point is Redmond on the eastern slope of the Cascades, or quite a bit longer if you are coming from points west and want to make more than a frenetic weekend of it. You can do a short loop, a long loop, or retrace your route if you didn't see enough of it the first time through. I'll leave the exact itinerary up to you, but hopefully, the following description will give you the initial inspiration to pack up and go!

The drive takes you along one of Oregon's most prized trout streams, over two historic and scenic mountain passes, through a diverse assortment of picturesque landscapes ranging from alpine meadows to high-desert grasslands, past many unusual geologic formations, across two of the state's largest national forests, and between two designated wilderness areas. All highways en route are designated National Scenic Byways.

To get there, begin the trip either in Eugene or Redmond on SR 126 (McKenzie Highway). The focal point of this excursion is between the towns of McKenzie Bridge and Sisters over State Routes 126, 20, and 242. You'll be better off if you simply remember these three road numbers (or have a state map with you), because the road names—McKenzie Highway, Santiam Highway, Belknap Springs Highway—don't always correspond to the same continuous stretch of road.

At any rate, the McKenzie River is the main feature in the western sector of the drive. Trail Bridge Campground is located on Trail Bridge Reservoir, a small depository of McKenzie River headwaters and a good stopping point in the journey.

Flowing pure and cold out of Clear Lake (a natural lava-dam lake just west of lava beds contained

RATINGS

Beauty: ✿ ✿ ✿
Privacy: ✿ ✿ ✿
Spaciousness: ✿ ✿ ✿
Quiet: ✿ ✿ ✿
Security: ✿ ✿ ✿
Cleanliness: ✿ ✿ ✿ ✿
Cleanliness: ✿ ✿ ✿ ✿

within Mount Jefferson Wilderness), the McKenzie River attracts both the drift-boat community and vast numbers of rafters, kayakers, and canoeists, who appreciate the McKenzie's gentle grade. In the entire boatable length of the river, there is only one Class IV rapid. The rest are Class I or II.

Fishing the McKenzie can induce even the toughest angler to near-poetic descriptions of his or her experience. Besides healthy runs of summer steelhead and spring chinook and a constant supply of hatchery rainbows, the McKenzie is idolized for its native son, the redside rainbow trout. In order to keep this species alive and flourishing in its natural environs, fishing regulations require that all rainbows over 14 inches be released. Native trout are identified by their ventral fin still intact; hatchery varieties will have theirs clipped. If you plan to do some fishing, check with authorities on current regulations.

Taking Belknap Springs Highway (continuing as SR 126) north from McKenzie Bridge, you'll encounter Trail Bridge Reservoir and the campground. If you choose to do the loop in reverse, turn right just before Belknap Springs onto SR 242, which is the continuation of McKenzie Highway. Here the road leaves the McKenzie and picks up the western border of Three Sisters Wilderness Area as it works its way along a series of hair-raising, hairpin turns to 5,342-foot McKenzie Pass.

Continuing east, the road drops down into Sisters, a ranch town prospering largely on tourism these days thanks to its unlimited recreational opportunities, moderate climate, and beautiful scenery. At Sisters, you'll catch up with the other half of SR 126, and you can continue straight across to Redmond. To finish the loop and to return to Trail Bridge Campground, turn northwest onto Santiam Highway (SR 126/US 20). Black Butte, a prominent natural point of interest with Metolius Spring at its base (see Riverside Campground page 85), is about 8 miles up the road on the right.

The road swings due west just beyond Black Butte, crossing Santiam Pass in about 6 more miles. The old Santiam Wagon Road was an alternative to the

KEY INFORMATION

ADDRESS: Trail Bridge Campground c/o McKenzie Ranger District 57600 McKenzie Highway McKenzie Bridge, OR 97413

OPERATED BY: Willamette National Forest

INFORMATION: (541) 822-3381

OPEN: Main season, April to September; open in off-season with no fees and no services

SITES: 26 tent sites; overflow primitive areas on flats near reservoir

EACH SITE HAS: Picnic table, fire grill, shade trees

ASSIGNMENT: First-come, first-served; no reservations

REGISTRATION: Self-registration on site

FACILITIES: Vault and seasonal flush toilets, piped water, boat dock nearby, limited disabled access

PARKING: At campsites

FEE: $6, $3 per additional vehicle

ELEVATION: 2,400 feet

RESTRICTIONS: Pets: On leash only
Fires: In fire pits only
Alcohol: Permitted
Vehicles: 45-foot trailer size limit
Other: Check for fishing regulations

MAP

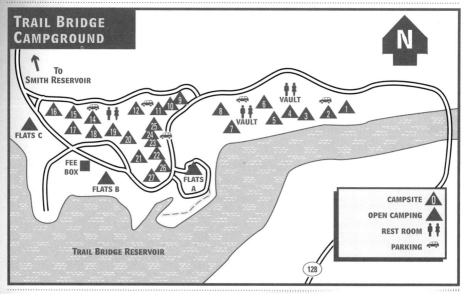

TRAIL BRIDGE CAMPGROUND

To SMITH RESERVOIR

FLATS C

FEE BOX

FLATS B

FLATS A

VAULT

VAULT

TRAIL BRIDGE RESERVOIR

128

N

CAMPSITE

OPEN CAMPING

REST ROOM

PARKING

GETTING THERE

Take SR 126 from Eugene or Redmond to McKenzie Bridge. Follow this road north; it becomes SR 26 (the continuation of Belknap Springs Highway) in McKenzie Bridge. Continue driving to Trail Bridge Reservoir and the campground.

McKenzie Pass route for pioneers heading farther north. If you hike the Pacific Crest Trail south from its intersection with US 20 for about 5 miles, you'll come to the original old road.

The final part of the loop turns southwest at Santiam Junction (roughly 6 miles from the pass) and then due south on SR 126 (Belknap Springs Highway), passing Fish Lake, Clear Lake, Smith Reservoir, and a series of falls.

If time allows or you have factored at least one hike into your schedule, sample a piece of the McKenzie River National Recreation Trail, easily accessed at Trail Bridge Campground. The trail doesn't leave the riverbank for much of its 26 miles and, aside from the pure delight of the McKenzie itself, offers such sights as rustic log bridges, primeval Douglas firs, magnificent waterfalls, and ancient lava beds.

TUMALO STATE PARK CAMPGROUND

FOR ME, THREE DAYS AT Tumalo State Park turned out to be one of the few luxurious extended stays I allowed myself in a madcap summer and fall of feverish campground research. So, if you're in the mood for a little extra campground comfort and want a well-managed compound with excellent facilities, peace of mind when daytripping, and location, location, location, you absolutely cannot beat Tumalo.

For certain, there will be RVs here, but Tumalo does offer a separate tent-camping area (although I think it could use improvement, if that's the right word). The tent camping loop is to the left of the ranger office as you enter the campground driveway. It's a rather small area by comparison to the Loops B and C above, but the tent sites are closest to the Deschutes River, which makes the environment seem more natural. However, the sites themselves are basic, fairly tight together, don't offer a lot of privacy as result of their adjacency, and have awkwardly situated tent pads in many cases.

In general, Loop A, seems mostly like an afterthought and a weak attempt to provide non-RVers with a home of their own. I'd like to see park administrators convert a portion of the day use area across O.B. Riley Road to tent camping. Where the day use area sprawls in grassy and shady opulence along the banks of the Deschutes (but is often empty), the tent camping area is squeezed.

Up above in the main camp complex, there are two loops, and if possible, it's best to grab a spot on the outside loop for more privacy. Don't plan on many spaces being available on short notice on summer weekends. If you know the dates you expect to be in the Bend area, it's best to make a reservation. However, there is a new, very specific cancellation policy in

> *Go ahead. Indulge yourself. You have my permission, and Tumalo is the place to do it.*

RATINGS

Beauty: ✰ ✰ ✰
Privacy: ✰ ✰
Spaciousness: ✰ ✰ ✰ ✰
Quiet: ✰ ✰
Security: ✰ ✰ ✰ ✰ ✰
Cleanliness: ✰ ✰ ✰ ✰ ✰
Insect control: ✰ ✰ ✰ ✰

ADDRESS: Tumalo State Park
62976 O.B. Riley
Road
Bend, OR 97701

OPERATED BY: Oregon State Parks

INFORMATION: (541) 388-6055;
www.oregon
stateparks.org

OPEN: Year-round

SITES: 58

EACH SITE HAS: Picnic table, fire
grill; some shade
trees

ASSIGNMENT: First come, first
served or by reserva-
tion (recommended
in high season) at
(800) 452-5687 or
www.reserveamer-
ica.com

REGISTRATION: Self registration on
site

FACILITIES: Flush toilets, separate solar-powered
shower building,
playground, fire-
wood and ice for
sale; 23 full-hookup
RV sites, 7 yurts, 2
group tent areas,
hiker/biker camp

PARKING: At campsites

FEE: $17, $21 full-hookup,
$4 hiker/biker; yurts
$27; $7 per addi-
tional vehicle

ELEVATION: 4,500 feet

RESTRICTIONS: Pets: On leash only
Fires: In fire grills
only
Alcohol: Permitted
at campsites only
Vehicles: 30-foot RV
size limit
Other: 14-day stay
limit

the Oregon campground system. Remember to have the cancellation terms clarified when making your reservation.

By the way, Tumalo has the distinction of being one of the few campgrounds in this book where a reservation is possible. Most of them are first come, first served. There's something about making a reservation to go camping that just seems odd to me. Of course, I'm not big on hotel reservations, either . . .

In fact, it was a lack of a reservation that got me in trouble at Tumalo right off the bat. I arrived with a plan to make Tumalo my base camp for exploring the numerous more rustic tent-camping options in the vicinity—and maybe cram in a golf game at a particular course I had heard good things about. I was hoping to stay five days.

I decided to indulge in the ultimate base camp luxury and sprung for a yurt for the first time (to report to my readers, of course). Since these semipermanent structures are the newest, hottest novelty in Northwest campgrounds, they get scooped up fast. Somehow, I managed to find yurt availability for three consecutive nights. Surely the work of the camping gods because on the fourth day, they conferred again and agreed, "Don't be greedy. You're outta here!" My yurt days may have been short-lived, but my regard for the structures is long-term. They are deserving of every accolade they receive, and may be the affordable answer when good tent camping goes bad.

Fortunately, I was able to complete my research in time and determined that Tumalo was, indeed, an ideal base camp for dandy expeditions in all direc-tions. A morning hike up above Tumalo Falls, an afternoon mountain-bike ride along the Metolius River, an evening gawk at the sunset from Smith Rock, a nighttime frolic in a Bend pub (I said this was my indulgent stint).

Aside from a surplus of RVs (which is every developed campground's plight in my estimation) and an uninspiring tent camping loop, the only notable drawback to Tumalo is the road noise from US 20. It carries over the treetops and above the Deschutes canyon, settling on the campground. Long-haul trucks

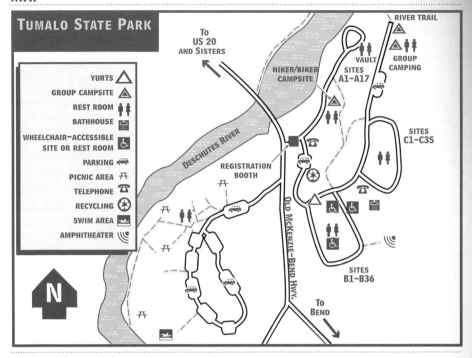

TUMALO STATE PARK

To
US 20
AND SISTERS

RIVER TRAIL

YURTS

GROUP CAMPSITE

REST ROOM

BATHHOUSE

WHEELCHAIR−ACCESSIBLE
SITE OR REST ROOM

PARKING

PICNIC AREA

TELEPHONE

RECYCLING

SWIM AREA

AMPHITHEATER

HIKER/BIKER
CAMPSITE

VAULT
SITES
A1−A17

GROUP
CAMPING

SITES
C1−C35

DESCHUTES RIVER

REGISTRATION
BOOTH

SITES
B1−B36

OLD MCKENZIE−BEND HWY.

To
BEND

N

ferrying goods east and west across the Cascades travel SR 20 with great regularity—and at all hours of the day and night. On a stiller than still night, the truck sounds are a reminder that Tumalo is not necessarily tent camping at its finest, but maybe at its most convenient. And sometimes, that's just what you need.

P.S.: I am eternally grateful to Rich and Val Allyn, camp hosts in the summer of 2003, for making my stay at Tumalo a hilarious and productive time.

GETTING THERE

From Bend, take US 20 west towards Sisters. Turn left on Old Redmond-Bend Highway. Turn right on O.B. Riley Road (also known as Old McKenzie–Bend Highway) and wind your way through a few sharp corners and sudden drops. At night, this little stretch of road is surprisingly dark. The campground entrance is on the right just before crossing the bridge over the Deschutes River. Total driving distance from intersection of US 97 and SR 20 in Bend is roughly 5 miles.

Prineville

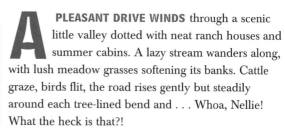

WILDCAT CAMPGROUND

> *A small and lightly traveled territory, Mill Creek Wilderness is right ouside your tent's back flap with a variety of hiking options and minus the crowds.*

A **PLEASANT DRIVE WINDS** through a scenic little valley dotted with neat ranch houses and summer cabins. A lazy stream wanders along, with lush meadow grasses softening its banks. Cattle graze, birds flit, the road rises gently but steadily around each tree-lined bend and . . . Whoa, Nellie! What the heck is that?!

The sight of lonely Steins Pillar rising 350 feet above the treetops across the valley is not quite what you'd expect in an otherwise pastoral scene, but there it is. A rather prominent vestige of ancient volcanic activity exposed after millions of years of wear and tear, Steins Pillar seems almost comically out of place. Unlike its counterparts, Twin Pillars and Whistler Peak, it was the unwitting victim of bad location when the Mill Creek Wilderness was formed by the 1984 Oregon Wilderness Act. All those years standing out there by itself and it turns out to be only 3 miles shy of where they drew the boundary line! It's unfortunate that there wasn't a way to include Steins Pillar within the protected area. I'll have to ask a ranger for the story, or maybe you can find out for me.

You can view Steins Pillar from a wayside pullover on Mill Creek Road, but there's a fair amount of private land between you and the spire. It takes the right kind of lens to capture the enormity of the pillar on film from this vantage point. If you want to take the detour to view Steins Pillar up close before continuing on up to Wildcat, look for the Steins Pillar sign about a mile past where Mill Creek Road turns to gravel. Turn right and follow this road sharply up for a little more than 2 miles. The hike in is about 2 miles as well and of average difficulty. Bring a water bottle.

Meanwhile, back at Wildcat . . . The campground is another 5 miles up Mill Creek Road and sits at the intersection of Mill Creek proper and its East Fork.

RATINGS

Beauty: ✿ ✿ ✿
Privacy: ✿ ✿ ✿ ✿
Spaciousness: ✿ ✿ ✿ ✿
Quiet: ✿ ✿ ✿ ✿ ✿
Security: ✿ ✿ ✿
Cleanliness: ✿ ✿ ✿
Insect control: ✿ ✿ ✿

The southwest boundary of the Mill Creek Wilderness is veritably at your tent's back flap. There is no other campground in this book that affords such close proximity to wilderness or so promotes a sense of quietude. Campsites are arranged in a loop with a blend of high desert grasses, aspen, and pines against a backdrop of sun-browned canyon slopes. With the East Fork of Mill Creek babbling through, it's quite a pretty, yet primitive setting. The locals will tell you this is one of the best places to cool off from the searing desert heat down below. Having driven in across east central Oregon's John Day River basin, I can wholeheartedly testify to that claim.

The higher you go, the cooler it will get. And the fewer people you'll find. The Mill Creek Wilderness is miniscule by comparison to most of Oregon's other wild lands, but it is the largest of three in the Ochoco Range (Bridge Creek and Black Canyon are the others). Despite this and its modest notoriety for quizzical rock formations, the Mill Creek Wlderness often gets overlooked by residents of the Bend/Redmond/Prineville metropolis, who typically migrate west into the Cascades or even further east into the heart of the Blue Mountains. The rock-climbing crowd has turned its fascination northwest to Smith Rock outside Terrebonne, and that reduces the public pressure on Mill Creek's attractions as well.

Given the small stature of the wilderness, its 21 miles of trails can be traversed in no time. On the other hand, once you're here, you might consider taking the opportunity to dawdle, since you're not required to canvass the land in record time. You'll get reasonable exercise, though, with three main trails in the system linking to each other in a range of elevations from 3,700 feet (at the campground) to as high as 6,200 feet.

And although it's cooler than the stifling desert, it's still plenty hot and dry, so carry lots of water.

A word of warning about the East Fork of Mill Creek and its tributaries while on the subject of water: Don't drink from the stream. It may look innocent enough—and how easy it would be to scoop up a palm-

KEY INFORMATION

ADDRESS: Wildcat Campground c/o Lookout Moutain Ranger District 3160 NE 3rd Street Prineville, OR 97754

OPERATED BY: Ochoco National Forest

INFORMATION: (541) 416-6500

OPEN: Mid-April to late October

SITES: 17

EACH SITE HAS: Picnic table, fire grill; some shade trees

ASSIGNMENT: First come, first served; no reservations

REGISTRATION: Self-registration on site

FACILITIES: Vault toilets, piped water

PARKING: At access road, 200–400 yards from campground

FEE: $8, $3 per additional vehicle

ELEVATION: 3,700 feet

RESTRICTIONS: **Pets:** On leash only **Fires:** In fire pits only **Alcohol:** Permitted **Vehicles:** 30-foot RV size limit, no hookups **Other:** 14-day stay limit

MAP

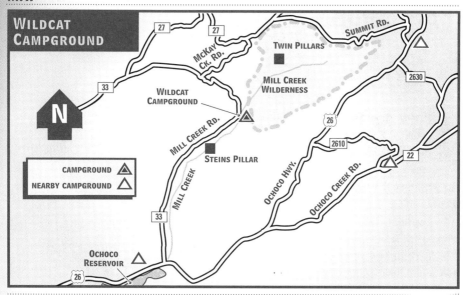

WILDCAT CAMPGROUND

27 27 SUMMIT RD. TWIN PILLARS ▲ 2630
McKAY CK. RD. MILL CREEK WILDERNESS
33 WILDCAT CAMPGROUND 26
N MILL CREEK RD. ▲ 2610 22
CAMPGROUND ▲ STEINS PILLAR OCHOCO HWY. OCHOCO CREEK RD. ▲
NEARBY CAMPGROUND ▲
MILL CREEK
33
OCHOCO RESERVOIR ▲
26

GETTING THERE

From Prineville, head east on US 26 for 9 miles to Mill Creek Road (FS 33). Turn left and follow the road for approximately 10 miles to the campground.

ful while you're heading up the trail to Twin Pillars. But keep in mind that free-ranging cattle are allowed inside the boundaries of Mill Creek and they have proven to be a nuisance to the natural environment, including the water.

Hopefully, you'll see more wildlife than cattle in your rambles through Mill Creek Wilderness. It's likely that you will, as the level of human traffic is not heavy enough to make native creatures unduly wary. You'd probably rather not run into a black bear or mountain lion (although both live here), but you may be lucky enough to glimpse elk, mule deer, and a variety of birds—the pileated woodpecker thrives on fallen old-growth ponderosas here, and wild turkeys roam the lower elevations.

YELLOWBOTTOM CAMPGROUND

I F YOU PLAN TO CAMP AT Yellowbottom and you want to take the scenic route first, come in from the US 22 connector on FS 11. This brings you along the ridge-running, breathtaking Quartzville Backcountry Byway, allegedly one of the least traveled byways in Oregon.

I certainly can't argue with that. When I made the crossing in late August, I passed a handful of cars and only encountered anything close to "busy" when I got beyond Yellowbottom and close to Green Peter Reservoir on the route's western end. The previous day, I had been subjected to the insult of major crowds at Olallie Lake, so I was particularly in need of a lonely drive to restore my faith.

If for no other reason than simply as a tribute to the collection of public and private interests working cooperatively to manage this region, the Quartzville Creek Corridor passes with flying colors. What other 50-mile stretch qualifies as dam-controlled, wild and scenic, historic, and recreational under the auspices of five different agencies? This alone is a modern miracle.

Yellowbottom Campground sits nearly equidistant from both ends of the Quartzville Byway and is the only developed campground within the Wild and Scenic portion of Quartzville Creek, falling under the Bureau of Land Management jurisdiction. Wedged into the right angle formed by Yellowbottom Creek falling from the north and Quartzville Creek running in an east-west parallel with the road, the campground has 21 sites laid out in an intelligent use of the natural geography. It is hard to find a site that seems inappropriate or awkwardly placed. The entire compound evokes simultaneously backcountry wildness and sense of order that is classic BLM—something to do with that "less is more" approach to recreational resources.

> *The only developed campground within the Wild and Scenic corridor of Quartzville Creek.*

RATINGS

Beauty: ✿ ✿ ✿ ✿ ✿
Privacy: ✿ ✿ ✿
Spaciousness: ✿ ✿ ✿ ✿ ✿
Quiet: ✿ ✿ ✿ ✿ ✿
Security: ✿ ✿ ✿ ✿ ✿
Cleanliness: ✿ ✿ ✿ ✿ ✿
Insect control: ✿ ✿ ✿

ADDRESS: Yellowbottom Campground c/o Tillamook Recreation Area Salem District Office 1717 Fabry Road SE Salem, OR 97306

OPERATED BY: Bureau of Land Management

INFORMATION: (503) 375-5646

OPEN: Mid-May to October

SITES: 20

EACH SITE HAS: Picnic table, fire grill, shade trees

ASSIGNMENT: First come, first served; no reservations

REGISTRATION: Self-registration on site

FACILITIES: Vault toilets, piped water, garbage service, firewood for purchase, camp host

PARKING: At campsites

FEE: $8; $5 per additional vehicle

ELEVATION: 1,500 feet

RESTRICTIONS: Pets: On leash only
Fires: In fire pits only
Alcohol: Permitted
Vehicles: No restrictions
Other: 14-day stay limit; no gathering wood gathering larger than 1-inch in diameter; entrance gate locked at 10 p.m.

Even so, this is one of the more developed BLM campgrounds I came across in my research travels. One would have to refer to Yellowbottom as practically upscale in comparison to most, and this is where the sense of order is evident. There is a woodshed for firewood. There is a pump house for water. There is a power building—for powering what I don't know. There is even a small cabin from which the camp host (who is only on site for the month of August) distributes literature. Neatly distant across the Quartzville Road from the overnight camping is the day-use/picnic area, which can be a bit of a hubbub on a sultry summer afternoon. Word has spread of the spectacular swimming hole on the Quartzville here. Bodies sprawl on every available sun-warmed rock surface after a quick plunge in becomes an even quicker scramble out. The Quartzville is clear, clear, clear but cold, cold, cold.

For a campground that sports an odd level of organization, the basic amenities (two sets of vault toilets) are not exactly situated in the best proximity to most of the campsites (it can be a long walk in the middle of the night, in other words). The same goes for the piped water. While the best sites for privacy are those backed up against the north slope of the campground (4, 5, 6, 8, 9, 11), they are the ones where you'll want to consider filling up one container and emptying another (if you know what I mean) before the campfires die out.

Old growth fir and western red cedar and rhododendron are the most noticeable permanent residents around Yellowbottom. The Rhododendron Trail, which loops around the north side of the campground boundary, is evidence of their peaceful coexistence and can be observed with a short but robust hike. Longer hikes are not far away in the petite and little-traveled Middle Santiam Wilderness. Here, anything but petite, is believed to be the largest remaining stand of old-growth forest in the western Cascades. Consider that piece of information for a minute or two. If you don't make it there on this trip, make sure you put that on your list of things to do sometime next year. The trailhead into the northern sector of the Middle Santiam is accessed off of FS 1142, a left-hand turn not more than 2 miles east of Yellowbottom.

MAP

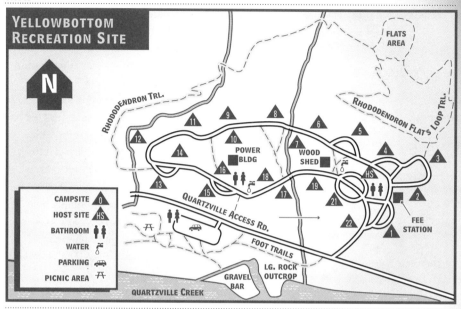

YELLOWBOTTOM RECREATION SITE

N

FLATS AREA

RHODODENDRON TRL.

RHODODENDRON FLATS LOOP TRL.

11   9   8

12   10   6

POWER BLDG   7 WOOD SHED   5

14   4   3

16   HS

13   18

15   17   19   2

QUARTZVILLE ACCESS RD.   21

22   FEE STATION

1

FOOT TRAILS

CAMPSITE	0
HOST SITE	HS
BATHROOM	
WATER	
PARKING	
PICNIC AREA	

GRAVEL BAR   LG. ROCK OUTCROP

QUARTZVILLE CREEK

The Quartzville Corridor is truly a gold mine (literally and figuratively), laden with opportunity whether your visit is an afternoon drive, a day picking huckleberries, an overnight gathering around a campfire, a week lost among old-growth giants, or a lifetime of trips, each with something different to offer. Gold mining put this area on the map once and still lures today's amateur fortune-hunters. Primarily, however, it has become the domain of fishermen, boaters, hikers and berrypickers. For the future, let's hope the legacies we have kept alive and the ones we have created inspire those that follow us.

GETTING THERE

From Sweet Home on US 20 east of Corvallis, turn left (north) on the Quartzville Road (FS 11) and follow it for 24 miles to the campground, which will be on your left. A day-use area and Quartzville Creek are on your right. You can also follow the Quartzville Road west from its eastern connection with OR 22.

SOUTHERN CASCADES AND ENVIRONS

FOURMILE LAKE CAMPGROUND

VIEWS OF A **9,500-FOOT** snowcapped peak. Spacious, lakefront tent sites wonderfully free of annoying mosquitoes. A wilderness boundary veritably at the backflap of your tent. Trailheads to some of the wildest high-elevation territory in Oregon. A vast national wildlife refuge less than 20 miles away. Regular security patrols. The services of civilization within an hour's drive.

It's hard to beat this glowing set of credentials, which is all part of the package when you stay at Fourmile Lake Campground in Winema National Forest.

Although Fourmile's campsites are sizable enough to accommodate RVs, the general sense of the place is one of solitude and serenity. This is due, in part, to the proximity of Sky Lakes Wilderness, whose boundary is outlined by nearly three-fourths of the lake's shoreline.

Creating this squiggly crook in the wilderness's otherwise linear demarcation, Fourmile Lake itself is not within the protected boundaries, and motorized boat travel (with enforced speed limits) is acceptable. Any form of mechanized transportation within the wilderness territory is, however, strictly prohibited.

As always when hiking into wilderness backcountry, it is a good idea to carry a compass and a detailed USGS topographic map of the area. Forest Service maps are generally reliable but are often not updated frequently enough to reflect the most recent additions or changes in their vast network of roads. Try to get the most current information from a Forest Service representative. They're very friendly and helpful in Klamath Falls.

Hiking is required to enjoy this area properly, so carefully consider your options in either Sky Lakes Wilderness or Mountain Lakes Wilderness. Trails into Sky Lakes begin very near the campground. The one to the northwest passes diminutive Squaw Lake (where

> *If you're campground shopping in the southern Oregon Cascades, it's hard to beat these fabulous views, lakefront sites, and wilderness trails.*

RATINGS

Beauty: ✿ ✿ ✿ ✿
Privacy: ✿ ✿ ✿
Spaciousness: ✿ ✿ ✿ ✿ ✿
Quiet: ✿ ✿ ✿ ✿
Security: ✿ ✿ ✿ ✿
Cleanliness: ✿ ✿ ✿ ✿ ✿
Insect control: ✿ ✿ ✿ ✿

ADDRESS: Fourmile Lake
Campground
c/o Klamath Ranger
District
1936 California
Avenue
Klamath Falls, OR
97601

OPERATED BY: Concessionaire for
Winema National
Forest

INFORMATION: (541) 885-3400

OPEN: Late June through
mid-October,
weather permitting

SITES: 25

EACH SITE HAS: Picnic table, fire pit
with grill, shade
trees

ASSIGNMENT: First come, first
served; no reserva-
tions

REGISTRATION: Self-registration on
site

FACILITIES: Pit toilets, central
hand pump for
water, boat launch

PARKING: At campsites

FEE: $8, $4 per additional
vehicle

ELEVATION: 5,800 feet

RESTRICTIONS: Pets: On leash only
Fires: In fire pits
only
Alcohol: Permitted
Vehicles: Not
allowed in wilder-
ness area; nonmotor-
ized boats only
Other: 14-day stay
limit

views of Mount McLoughlin will make you stop and gawk) and soon thereafter connects with the Pacific Crest National Scenic Trail (about 2 miles from the campground). From there, you could hike south on the Pacific Crest Trail to its junction with the Mount McLoughlin Trail (a difficult but nontechnical climb). The summit is about 3 miles from this point. The trip from campground to peak would make for a rather rigorous 14-mile, round-trip day hike. The alternative is to hike the Mount McLoughlin Trail from its trailhead on FS 3650. An elevation gain of 4,000 feet doesn't make the trip any easier, but it is shorter (10 miles round-trip). Be sure to read the brochure that is provided at the trailhead. It covers some necessary precautions that can make the difference between delight and disaster on this fourth-highest Oregon Cascade volcano.

To experience the true essence of Sky Lakes Wilderness, I recommend driving to the Cold Springs trailhead on FS 3651. Saunter into the heart of this magnificent area with Imagination Peak as your inspiration. Beginning at an altitude of 5,800 feet, the trail climbs gently up and down without general elevation gain or loss.

In about 6 miles, you'll come to Heavenly Twin Lakes and the turnaround point if you're just out for the day. This is a good spot to see osprey that travel from nesting areas up to 8 miles away to fish in the hundreds of lakes scattered in this alpine basin. The trail wanders north past more peaks and lakes until it catches up with the Pacific Crest Trail as it works its way toward Crater Lake National Park.

South and east of Fourmile Lake is Mountain Lakes Wilderness, one of the oldest designated wilderness areas in Oregon and, for that matter, the entire country. The Forest Service included it in its Primitive Areas designations back in the 1930s, and it was incorporated under the 1964 Wilderness Act. Lesser known than the more popular destinations to the north but quite accessible from a trailhead at Sunset Campground, it may be the ticket for those seeking more solitary environs.

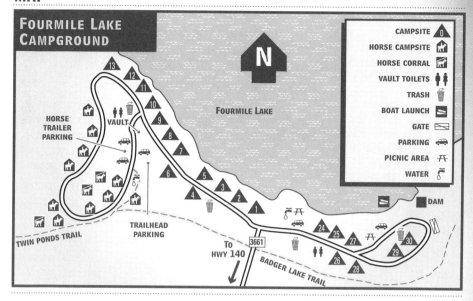

A challenging side trip—if you have the four-wheel rig to make it—is up Pelican Butte (also accessed from FS 3651). The Forest Service once manned a lookout station here, but the road is not maintained for normal-clearance vehicles. Currently, Pelican Butte is officially designated as an 11,000-acre roadless area but a wilderness status is pending. No word on when this may be approved, but there is no doubt it would be a good thing for nature lovers.

Of course, hiking is not the only way to see this spectacular region. Rent a canoe down on Pelican Bay and follow Upper Klamath Canoe Trail through 6 miles of lake and marshland. An array of wildlife and waterfowl inhabit the 15,000 acres that comprise the Klamath National Wildlife Refuge

GETTING THERE

Take SR 140 (Lake of the Woods Highway) northwest out of Klamath Falls for 38 miles, then turn right onto FS 3661, and head north for 5.5 miles to the campground. From Medford, head east on SR 140 for 40 miles. From this direction, you will turn left onto FS 3661.

HEAD OF THE RIVER CAMPGROUND

A great little out-of-the-way place where you'll run into more wildlife than people.

WE WERE SITTING in a coffee shop in Klamath Falls, hard on the campground research trail. Besides the aroma of fresh-ground French roast opening up my drowsy, sleep-stagnant eyes, there was the unmistakable scent of a soon-to-be-discovered campground. You know, one of the campgrounds that the locals are afraid to tell anyone about—either because they fear the Forest Service will get wind of it and "undevelop" it to death or some sly, yuppie outdoor writer (hey, not me!) will want to tell the whole world about it.

As it turns out, my hunch was right. How do I get so lucky? You learn to recognize the signals quickly.

"Say, you wouldn't happen to know of any great little out-of-the-way camping spots around here, would you?" I asked innocently, with my nose stuck in a steaming mug.

The place wasn't very crowded, so it was obvious to the fellow behind the counter that the question was meant for him. He looked up with the tiniest twist of a smile, cocked his head to the side in exaggerated contemplation, pursed his lips, and said, "What do you mean by 'out of the way?'"

He then told me about this dandy little spot known as Head of the River Campground. Lo and behold, I had actually seen it listed on campground lists—I guess I wasn't the first to play that game with the Klamath coffee connoisseur. They must have some arrangement with the Forest Service.

There isn't much to lure campers out to this tableland of ponderosa pine, lodgepole pine, and other conifers except a bit of excellent trout fishing in the Williamson River and a crazy contingent of Forest Service roads wandering in and around the numerous buttes and flats. The Forest Service would like to encourage more recreational use of these roads, which

RATINGS

Beauty: ✿ ✿ ✿ ✿
Privacy: ✿ ✿
Spaciousness: ✿ ✿ ✿ ✿
Quiet: ✿ ✿ ✿ ✿
Security: ✿ ✿
Cleanliness: ✿ ✿ ✿
Insect control: ✿ ✿ ✿

are primarily used by loggers. Problem is, they're too busy attending to the demands of campers in the over-run areas and don't have the budget to promote less-trammeled spots. When I talked with employees at both Chiloquin and Klamath Ranger Stations (Head of the River is located in the Chiloquin District but Klamath purports to manage it), they were polite and helpful from start to finish but scratched their heads at the notion that anyone would consider Head of the River and the surrounding terrain a place to seek out. But intrepid campers may be pleasantly surprised.

This area is relatively dry year-round, and the only substantial precipitation comes in the form of snow at higher elevations. However, enough ground-water seeps to the surface from natural springs (this is precisely the case with the headwaters of the Williamson) that wildflowers, such as fireweed, fox-glove, lupine, and dandelion, define the banks of tiny, short-lived creeks every spring.

You'll most likely encounter more wildlife than fellow campers out here. More than 230 species of birds and 80 varieties of mammals inhabit the region. In the summer months, watch out for rattlesnakes and bring your mosquito repellent. Carry your own drink-ing water to Head of the River or be prepared to treat what you take from the river.

Rather than backtracking along the route you take to reach this pristine spot, consider a loop trip by contin-uing north on Williamson River Road, which becomes Silver Lake Road just above the expansive Klamath Marsh. You can get a close-up views of Klamath National Wildlife Refuge because Silver Lake Road cuts a diagonal across the refuge's midsection to a juncture with US 97 at Chinchalo. This could easily be one of the least-traveled byways you'll find in this book.

All in all, this is a remote area that begs to be appreciated simply for . . . well, its simplicity. The campground is as primitive as they come, with only five sites, no piped water, and no fee. For more specifics on the area, check either with the Chiloquin or Klamath Ranger District.

KEY INFORMATION

ADDRESS: Head of the River Campground c/o Chiloquin Ranger District 38500 Highway 97 North Chiloquin, OR 97624

OPERATED BY: Winema National Forest, Klamath Ranger District

INFORMATION: (541) 783-4001

OPEN: May to October, weather permitting

SITES: 6

EACH SITE HAS: Picnic table, shade trees

ASSIGNMENT: First come, first served; no reserva-tions

REGISTRATION: Not necessary

FACILITIES: Wheelchair-accessible vault toi-lets, firewood, no piped water

PARKING: At campsites

FEE: No fee

ELEVATION: 4,500 feet

RESTRICTIONS: Pets: On leash only
Fires: In fire pits only
Alcohol: Permitted
Vehicles: 30-foot RV size limit

MAP

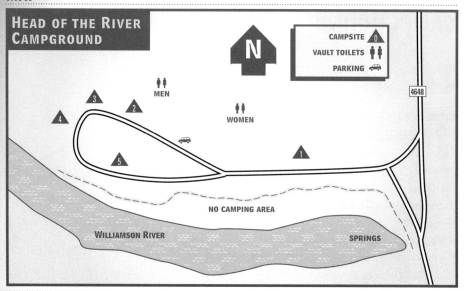

HEAD OF THE RIVER CAMPGROUND

N

CAMPSITE ▲0
VAULT TOILETS ♀♀
PARKING 🚗

MEN ♀♀

▲3
▲2
▲4

WOMEN ♀♀

🚗

▲5

▲1

4648

NO CAMPING AREA

WILLIAMSON RIVER

SPRINGS

GETTING THERE

Take Sprague River Highway (OR 858) northeast out of Chiloquin. Take a left onto Williamson River Highway just beyond the 5-mile point. Follow this road 27 miles to the access road, FS 4648. Take a left; the campground is 1 mile on the left. Signs for the campground begin at the turn for FS 4648.

LOST CREEK CAMPGROUND

THERE'S ONE THING I NEED to say right away about Lost Creek Campground: Get there as early as possible and stake your claim. Bribe somebody if you have to.

Here's the deal. Lost Creek is only one of two campgrounds inside the boundary of Crater Lake National Park. And with 16 tent-only sites—compared to Mazama's 198 multipurpose sites—the odds are not in a latecomer's favor. Even though Lost Creek is a bit off the beaten path, the area is swarming with people looking for overnight accommodations—roughly half a million visitors per year at last count. Many of them come from around the world. As acknowledgment of this, the park service offers trip-planning information in German, Spanish, and French on its Web site. I even encountered two German bicyclists who flew to Montana and were pedaling to Los Angeles via Crater Lake. I hope they made it. Nice to have so many cultures converging in such an unspoiled spot, actually. Natural beauty may make the best ambassador.

Oregon's only national park, which turned 100 years old in 2002, retains the stupendous natural wonders that garnered its protection in 1902. Park staff today feel that William Steel, the singular driving force behind the park's creation then, would be impressed with how little Crater Lake has changed in the course of a century. Besides the paving of formerly dirt roads, the only evident change is at Crater Lake Lodge, which underwent a multimillion-dollar remodeling in the early 1990s.

If this is your first trip to Crater Lake National Park, be prepared. Your jaw will drop when you take your first peek over the rim of this massive caldera. Everyone has an opinion on the best spot for your first good gawk but, frankly, that's just splitting hairs. The

Jaw-dropping Crater Lake attracts an international crowd, so don't be surprised if your fellow campers don't speak English.

RATINGS

Beauty: ✰ ✰ ✰ ✰
Privacy: ✰ ✰ ✰ ✰ ✰
Spaciousness: ✰ ✰ ✰ ✰ ✰
Quiet: ✰ ✰ ✰ ✰ ✰
Security: ✰ ✰ ✰
Cleanliness: ✰ ✰ ✰ ✰
Insect control: ✰ ✰ ✰

ADDRESS: Lost Creek
Campground
Crater Lake
National Park
P.O. Box 7
Crater Lake, OR
97604

OPERATED BY: National Park Service

INFORMATION: (541) 594-2211,
ext. 402

OPEN: Early July to late
September, depending on snow level

SITES: 16

EACH SITE HAS: Picnic table, fire grill

ASSIGNMENT: First come, first
served; no reservations

REGISTRATION: Self-registration on
site

FACILITIES: Flush toilets, piped
water

PARKING: At campsites

FEE: $10

ELEVATION: 6,000 feet

RESTRICTIONS: Pets: On leash only
Fires: In fire pits
only
Alcohol: At campsites only
Vehicles: Motorbikes
allowed; no accommodations for RVs

deepest lake in the United States, the second deepest in North America, and the seventh deepest in the world, Crater Lake is the result of the cataclysmic eruption of Mount Mazama some 6,850 years ago. It once was a stratovolcano similar to Mount Hood and Mount Shasta and stood roughly a mile higher than the current lake level before it collapsed. There are several excellent publications about Crater Lake, Mount Mazama, and the park at the visitor center in Rim Village. I found it helpful to have these along as I toured the area. It's the kind of place where a little knowledge can make the trip immensely more pleasurable.

Rim Drive circumnavigates the perimeter of the 6-mile-wide lake for a total distance of 33.4 miles. There are numerous viewpoints along the way that will slow your driving time, but figure roughly two hours to complete the loop. In the winter, Rim Drive is open only between park headquarters and Rim Village, accessed by way of SR 62 from either the west or south. In all seasons, Rim Drive is open to mountain bikes, but there is no shoulder—so be careful!

Recreational activities in the 183,277 acres of Crater Lake National Park border on exhaustive, but the wanderer in you may want to simply observe on foot the diverse plant and animal life native to this part of Oregon. There are more than 140 miles of hiking trails (including a section of the Pacific Crest National Scenic Trail), and with so many of the park's visitors limiting their activity to areas closest to the crater's rim and park services, it is relatively easy to find solitude on a trail. Some trails reach elevations close to 9,000 feet and can take their toll on unconditioned legs and the unacclimatized cardiovascular system. Remember to carry water and take frequent rest stops to adjust to the altitude—and the incredibly fresh air.

For the geologist in you, there are destinations such as The Pinnacles (further up the road from Lost Creek Camp) and similarly weird formations on the Godfrey Glen Trail. The Pumice Desert is on the north side of the park, and Wizard Island, the small, symmetrical volcanic cone protruding from the lake, is accessible by boat from Cleetwood Cove. It's a steep, 720-foot drop on a trail just over a mile long to hike to the cove.

MAP

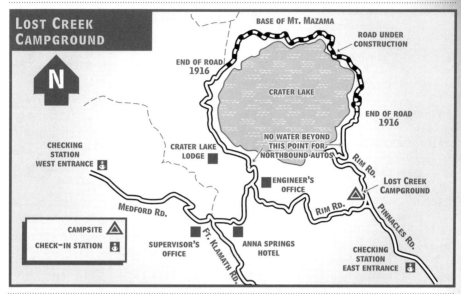

LOST CREEK CAMPGROUND

N

BASE OF MT. MAZAMA

ROAD UNDER CONSTRUCTION

END OF ROAD 1916

CRATER LAKE

END OF ROAD 1916

CHECKING STATION WEST ENTRANCE

CRATER LAKE LODGE

NO WATER BEYOND THIS POINT FOR NORTHBOUND AUTOS

RIM RD.

ENGINEER'S OFFICE

LOST CREEK CAMPGROUND

MEDFORD RD.

RIM RD.

PINNACLES RD.

CAMPSITE

CHECK-IN STATION

SUPERVISOR'S OFFICE

FT. KLAMATH RD.

ANNA SPRINGS HOTEL

CHECKING STATION EAST ENTRANCE

The way down may seem manageable enough, but after several hours of hiking on Wizard Island, that last mile back up may be the most memorable. Leave enough time to make the ascent in daylight.

Winter at Crater Lake is the dominant season, starting as early as October and lasting well into what is early summer in most places. Annual snowfall averages around 500 inches, which means endless winter-recreation opportunities if you're prepared. The park offers marked (but not groomed) cross-country skiing trails and snowmobile options. Most services in the park close in winter, but the cafe and gift shop at Rim Village stay open daily. Check the park's Web site for the most current conditions when considering a winter escape.

GETTING THERE

From Medford, follow SR 62 east for 77 miles and turn left at the Anna Springs Entrance. Continue past Mazama Campground to Rim Drive and turn right. Turn right at Kerr Notch toward The Pinnacles. Lost Creek Campground is adjacent to tiny Lost Creek several miles down this road.

Prospect

NATURAL BRIDGE CAMPGROUND

> *This is a good place to set up camp and explore the beautiful and often-overlooked Upper Rogue River area. Be sure to take a map!*

OFTEN OVERLOOKED BY travelers scurrying between the heavily promoted majesty of Crater Lake and the famed, lower Wild and Scenic Rogue River, the Upper Rogue River area offers its own style of spectacular scenery and wilderness treasures that should satisfy the desires of most outdoor adventurers.

If you're set on experiencing the beauty of the Rogue by boat, however, you'll be disappointed to discover that this section of the river is off limits to kayaks and canoes. Head on down to Grants Pass or the town of Rogue River, and they'll take care of you there.

Here, in Upper Rogue territory, the river plummets out of its source in Crater Lake National Park at a rate of as much as 48 feet per mile. Take a look down from precipitous heights along SR 62 north of Natural Bridge Campground for perhaps the clearest indication of why this portion of the river is so unrunnable. The flash of silver far below is the Rogue hurling itself seaward through the deep, narrow fissure known as the Rogue River Gorge.

Natural Bridge Campground is so named for the unique geological feature adjacent to it. In this location, the Upper Rogue disappears from sight and runs through an underground channel for 200 feet. The campground sits virtually atop the channel, with water flowing beneath it. A 2-mile interpretive loop trail explains the phenomenon.

Natural Bridge is one of several campgrounds in the vicinity located on the banks of the Rogue or on small creeks that feed it. Given its proximity to Crater Lake, this area can be quite busy in the summertime, but the larger, more developed campsites tend to fill up first. The lack of piped water or hookups at Natural Bridge discourages those who are not prepared for primitive conditions. The surrounding Rogue River

RATINGS

Beauty: ✿ ✿ ✿ ✿ ✿
Privacy: ✿ ✿ ✿ ✿ ✿
Spaciousness: ✿ ✿ ✿
Quiet: ✿ ✿ ✿ ✿
Security: ✿ ✿ ✿ ✿
Cleanliness: ✿ ✿ ✿ ✿ ✿
Insect control: ✿ ✿ ✿ ✿

National Forest is characterized by dense forests of Douglas fir and sugar pine, which soften the contours of the high plateau upon which they grow. More than 450 miles of trail within the national forest lead to remote high-country lakes, ridgetop vistas, and the secluded Rogue-Umpqua Divide Wilderness. Some of the routes connect with trails into the adjoining Umpqua National Forest.

Numerous day hikes and extended backpacking trips reveal not only the natural splendor of this undisturbed country but also the diverse wildlife and plant species that thrive in the moderate climate. The most famous inhabitant of Upper Rogue country is the northern spotted owl, which shares this lush expanse with an astonishing assortment of nocturnal creatures.

Except at the highest altitudes, which receive sizable measures of snow in the winter and stay cool year-round, the area enjoys warm and dry summers, with most of the 20 to 40 inches of annual precipitation occurring between October and May.

This rugged land is full of thick vegetation. Getting lost is easy. Make sure you have a good topographic or Forest Service map with you when you head out for lonely and distant spots. Booklets of maps and trail guides are available at the Rogue River National Forest headquarters in Medford or at the district office in Prospect.

If you are looking for an ambitious overland trek, take the Upper Rogue River Trail, which follows the river along its banks for 48 miles until it intersects with the Pacific Crest Trail in Crater Lake National Park. Starting in Prospect, the Upper Rogue Trail does not seem to attract as much print attention as its lower counterpart, known officially as the Rogue River National Recreation Trail. There's very little mention of the upper trail in regional guidebooks, so check in at the ranger station in Prospect, which is the best source for all outdoor recreation options in the area.

You can explore the trail in sections (who's got time for 48 miles all in one trip, anyway)? If you *do* have the time (and two cars or some kind of shuttle option), tackle the entire stretch and make daily desti-

KEY INFORMATION

ADDRESS:	Natural Bridge Campground c/o Prospect Ranger District 47201 Crater Lake Highway (SR 62) Prospect, OR 97536
OPERATED BY:	Rogue River National Forest
INFORMATION:	(541) 560-3400
OPEN:	Late May until snow forces closure (typically in early November)
SITES:	17
EACH SITE HAS:	Picnic table, fire pit with grill, shade trees
ASSIGNMENT:	First come, first served; no reservation
REGISTRATION:	Not necessary
FACILITIES:	Vault toilets, no piped water
PARKING:	At campsites
FEE:	$8, $4 per additional vehicle
ELEVATION:	3,200 feet
RESTRICTIONS:	Pets: On leash only Fires: In fire pits only Alcohol: Permitted Vehicles: 22-foot RV size limit

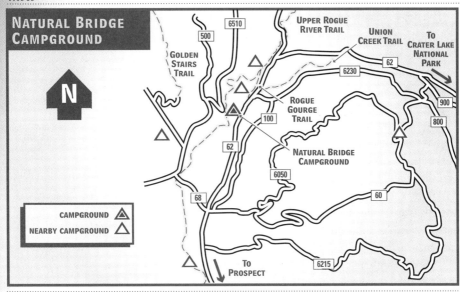

NATURAL BRIDGE CAMPGROUND

CAMPGROUND △

NEARBY CAMPGROUND △

GETTING THERE

Travel northeast on SR 62 (Crater Lake Highway) about 32 miles from Medford. From the Prospect turnoff, continue north on SR 62 another 11 miles or so to FS 300. Turn left, and the campground is 1 mile in. From Crater Lake, take SR 62 west if you are leaving the park from the south. If you exit from the north side, follow SR 138 to its intersection with SR 230. Head west and eventually south on SR 230 until it becomes SR 62. You'll turn right onto FS 300 about 3 miles from this point.

nations of the campgrounds sprinkled along the way, Natural Bridge included. This would be a fine way to spend a week getting intimately acquainted with the best of Upper Rogue country. For an even more unusual treat, try a bit of Nordic skiing along sections of the trail in winter. If you're a climber with Level 1–4 skills, you may want to test your ability on an odd geologic formation near the Rogue-Umpqua Divide Wilderness boundary. A pair of 400-foot spires known as Rabbit Ears, first climbed in 1921, continues to intrigue the adventuresome.

RUJADA CAMPGROUND

SOMETIMES, EVEN A tent-camping guidebook like this one needs to recognize that every outing can't be a week-long planning and preparation extravaganza. Sometimes, you just want a spot that doesn't require a tank of gas but still offers a rewarding wilderness experience. If you've only got a night to spare, welcome to Rujada. If you want to make it seem like a longer trip, head out there on your bicycle.

There is nothing particularly dramatic or exotic about Rujada. Except its name. Rujada, Rujada, Rujada. Don't have a clue what it means, but it rolls off the tongue in an alluring way. As you drive down the lane and cross the bridge over Layng Creek, you'll say "Hey, what a great little campground. Why haven't we been here before?"

A mere 20 miles or so east of Cottage Grove up the Row River Road (which turns into FS 17), Rujada sits alone in creekside luxury at the base of Rose Hill and just off the corner where a majority of the metropolitan crowd takes the right turn up Brice Creek Road to a host of much busier campgrounds. Rujada is located in the upper reaches of the Umpqua National Forest, a sprawling one million acres on the western slopes of the Cascades. The forest is characterized by the striking contrasts between cascading waterfalls, whitewater-river canyons, mountaintop vistas, and the ever-present green, green, green of ancient forests with shaggy coats of moss and lichen.

Rujada Campground is a microcosm of the Umpqua's ecosystems, with the clear and refreshing waters of Layng Creek at its feet, an expansive under-story of ferns skirting its boundaries, stands of second-growth Douglas fir scattered throughout, and two dramatic waterfalls a short distance up FS 17.

> *An easy place to reach for a quick overnight but with plenty of natural features nearby to satisfy your wilderness urges.*

RATINGS

Beauty: ✿ ✿ ✿
Privacy: ✿ ✿ ✿ ✿ ✿
Spaciousness: ✿ ✿ ✿ ✿ ✿
Quiet: ✿ ✿ ✿ ✿
Security: ✿ ✿ ✿ ✿ ✿
Cleanliness: ✿ ✿ ✿ ✿ ✿
Insect Control: ✿ ✿ ✿

ADDRESS: Rujada Campground c/o Cottage Grove Ranger District Brice Creek Recreation Corridor 40730 Layng Creek Road Culp Creek, OR 97427

OPERATED BY: Umpqua National Forest

INFORMATION: (541) 767-5000, (541) 942-5591

OPEN: Late May through September

SITES: 11

EACH SITE HAS: Picnic table, fire grill, shade trees

ASSIGNMENT: First come, first served; no reservations

REGISTRATION: Self-registration on site

FACILITIES: Flush and vault toilets, piped water, garbage service, playing field, camp host in high season

PARKING: At campsites

FEE: $7, $3 per additional vehicle

ELEVATION: 1,200 feet

RESTRICTIONS: **Pets:** On leash only **Fires:** In fire pits only **Alcohol:** Permitted **Vehicles:** 21-foot RV size limit, no hookups **Other:** 14-day stay limit

The campground is laid out in classic, circular fashion as was the trend when campgrounds (including this one) were first developed by the Civilian Conservation Corps back in the 1930s. Evidence of its early origins is displayed at the historic register booth in the picnic area.

Most of Rujada's 11 sites are tucked deep into vegetated pockets, affording the ultimate in privacy. Site 4 is the closest in proximity to a delightfully private swimming hole on the Layng that attracts day users as well as campers. Knowledge of this particular swimming hole must rely heavily on word-of-mouth, because if the camp host hadn't told me about it, I doubt if I would have found it on my own (there's nothing at the campground advertising it, and dense underbrush keeps it hidden). Each campsite has plenty of space for a large tent and is appointed with a standard but sturdy wooden picnic table with the well-worn look of camping days gone by. The fire pits are concrete rings with grates.

Rujada is not the kind of campground that invigorates the soul to robust activity. Rather, it's a place of relaxation and serenity with perhaps a smattering of youthful vigor in the adjoining playing field (although I'm not quite sure what level of demand there is for its use). The first choice of activity for overworked adults in the immediate vicinity is hiking the Swordfern Trail, an easy walk just over a mile that follows Layng Creek partway, overtakes an old abandoned logging road, and completes its loop near the picnic area. If you're inclined to do more than this, the two waterfalls farther up FS 17 are must-sees and require little effort to reach their ultimate rewards. Catch Spirit Falls in early afternoon for the best photographic light, as it stays shrouded in shadows most of the day. Moon Falls is best viewed during periods of late spring or early summer runoff when the 125-foot plummet is at full tilt.

If this isn't enough to fill up your weekend, a drive up to Fairview Lookout and Musick Guard Station offers superb views and a taste of history. On the clearest of days, both Mount Hood to the north and Mount Shasta in California can be seen. The guard

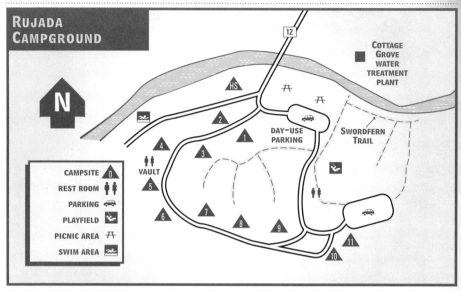

RUJADA CAMPGROUND

12

COTTAGE GROVE WATER TREATMENT PLANT

HS

DAY−USE PARKING

SWORDFERN TRAIL

VAULT

CAMPSITE	0
REST ROOM	♀♂
PARKING	🚗
PLAYFIELD	🏊
PICNIC AREA	⛺
SWIM AREA	🏊

station has been placed on the National Historic Register and the lookout (rebuilt in 1972) has served as fire lookout and radar receptor at different times in its past. Both the cabin and lookout tower are available to rent. Pick up brochures for both facilities at the campground.

If you have any time after these excursions, you may want to take the high-road route up and over Patterson Mountain that drops down into the Oakridge area. FS 17 switches to FS 5840 as it passes from Umpqua to Willamette National Forest, but I found my way to and from the Oakridge side with no problem. It's a little known back country drive that you can easily fit into a loose itinerary, and which may inspire you to return for another weekend.

GETTING THERE

From Cottage Grove, take Row River Road east for 19 miles to FS 17. Turn left and drive 2 miles to the campground entrance on the right. Cross Layng Creek and you're there.

SACANDAGA CAMPGROUND

> *Waldo Lake,*
> *Diamond Peak,*
> *and the Willamette*
> *River are all within*
> *easy reach of*
> *Sacandaga.*

THE AREA SURROUNDING Oakridge and West-fir is a forest playground for the outdoor-ori-ented masses of the Eugene-Springfield area. It is also becoming quite well-known (thanks in part to self-promotion) as a mountain-biking destination in the world beyond Oregon, but don't expect a hip, lively scene like that of other burgeoning Meccas for outdoor enthusiasts. It's still pretty quaint—which is not necessarily a bad thing! The number of churches outweighs the tavern listings on the Visitor's Map, if that tells you anything. I didn't spend too much time in town, but saw the standard assortment of modest local cafes and few fast-food eateries. I found good coffee (by Pacific Northwest standards) and pastries at The Trailhead Coffeehouse.

Oakridge is also a jumping-off point to High Cas-cades wonders in the southern Willamette National Forest, including Waldo Lake—one of the purest lakes in the world—and majestic Diamond Peak. Sacandaga Campground is close enough to town for conveniences but far enough away to be serene. It's safely away from the sometimes rowdy campers along nearby Hills Creek Reservoir and is definitely less overrun than supremely popular Waldo Lake, yet it's within day-tour driving distance of the High Cascades. At Sacandaga, the Middle Fork Willamette cuts through a narrow canyon that is seemingly far below but still emits up through the dense forest of Douglas fir, cedar, and hemlock one of the most pleasant campground sounds—the soothing constancy of a rushing river. A steep trail leads down to the river; walk cautiously in wet conditions, as it is easy to lose your footing.

At the campground itself, you'll find beautifully spacious campsites beneath a deep-forest canopy inter-spersed with dogwood trees. In my estimation, camp-sites 4, 6, and 8 are the best. Each sits on the edge of

RATINGS

Beauty: ✪ ✪ ✪ ✪ ✪
Privacy: ✪ ✪ ✪ ✪
Spaciousness: ✪ ✪ ✪ ✪ ✪
Quiet: ✪ ✪ ✪ ✪ ✪
Security: ✪ ✪ ✪ ✪
Cleanliness: ✪ ✪ ✪ ✪ ✪
Cleanliness: ✪ ✪ ✪

the bluff high above the river, the best vantage point for views and the sounds of the river right out of your tent door. Back in to your campsite, unload in relative privacy, and except for the occasional trip to the water faucet or the vault toilet, you can choose to have very little contact with other campers. Chances are these sites will be available, as the Forest Service rates this campground as seeing "low" usage, but you really can't go wrong anywhere within the camp if you don't get one of the prime spots.

Great driving tours are within easy reach of Sacandaga Campground, but one of the best tours can be enjoyed via foot, pedal, or hoof power right from the campground. The 27-mile-long Middle Fork Trail meanders through old-growth stands and meadows up and around the river, ending at the headwaters of its eponymous creek at Timpanogas Lake (see profile on page 125). The trail is open to hikers, horses, and mountain bikers; the lower part of the trail is considered a good introduction to serious mountain biking, with enough roots, rocks, and short climbs to challenge (but not discourage) a beginner. It also makes a great hike that even the youngest member of your party can enjoy. Sacandaga sits a little less than halfway along the trail, so you can choose routes in either direction.

Sections of the Middle Fork Trail follow the old Oregon Central Military Wagon Road, originally built in 1864 to bring cattle from the Willamette Valley over Emigrant Pass to the southern and eastern portions of the state. (It was eventually replaced by what is now OR 58 over Willamette Pass). The campground lies along the Diamond Drive Tour, which also follows part of the Military Wagon Road. The newly-designated route stretches south from Oakridge to SR 138 along the Rogue-Umpqua Scenic Byway, and provides excellent views of Diamond Peak, Mount Thielsen, and Sawtooth Mountain. Diamond Drive also connects on its north end to FS 19, also known as Aufderheide Scenic Byway. The Aufderheide tour starts near the longest covered bridge in Oregon, located in Westfir, and climbs along the rugged North Fork of the Middle Fork of the Willamette River, to the McKenzie River

KEY INFORMATION

ADDRESS:	Sacandaga Campground c/o Middle Fork Ranger District 46375 Oregon Highway 58 Westfir, OR 97492
OPERATED BY:	Willamette National Forest
INFORMATION:	(541) 782-2283
OPEN:	July through October
SITES:	17
EACH SITE HAS:	Picnic table, fire pit
ASSIGNMENT:	First-come, first-served; no reservations
REGISTRATION:	Self-registration on site
FACILITIES:	Vault toilets, piped water
PARKING:	At campsites
FEE:	$6, $3 per additional vehicle
ELEVATION:	2,400 feet
RESTRICTIONS:	**Pets:** On leash only **Fires:** In fire pits only **Alcohol:** Permitted **Vehicles:** 24-foot trailer size limit

MAP

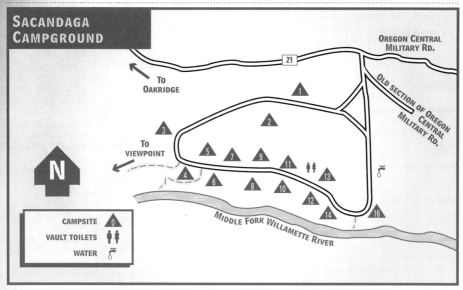

SACANDAGA CAMPGROUND

OREGON CENTRAL MILITARY RD.

21

To OAKRIDGE

OLD SECTION OF OREGON CENTRAL MILITARY RD.

1

2

3

To VIEWPOINT

5

7

9

11

13

N

4

6

8

10

12

14

16

MIDDLE FORK WILLAMETTE RIVER

CAMPSITE 0

VAULT TOILETS

WATER

GETTING THERE

From Oakridge (about 40 miles southeast of Eugene on SR 58), turn right on Kitson Springs Road, just east of town. Go half a mile and turn right on FS 21 (also known as Rigdon Road and Diamond Drive). Travel 26 miles to the campground, on your right.

and SR 126 (see Frissell Crossing, page 76, for more information on the Aufderheide).

Closer to the Oakridge end of FS 21, an alternative camping option, Larison Cove, is a canoe-in campground on a 1.5-mile-long arm of Hills Creek Reservoir, where motorized boats are prohibited. Of course, the likelihood of RVs at Larison Cove is fairly slim unless they now make them with pontoons! Four campsites include tables and fire rings in a quiet old-growth setting. Put-in at FS 2106, after about 3 miles on FS 21.

THIELSEN VIEW CAMPGROUND

THIELSEN **V**IEW **IS ONE** of several Forest Service campgrounds in the Diamond Lake vicinity, but it's somewhat removed from the mayhem of SR 138 because it sits alone on the western shore. With two other campgrounds across scenic Diamond Lake that can accommodate several hundred campers between them, chances are you won't find yourself alone out in this seemingly remote territory.

Diamond Lake is an immensely popular area, particularly for trout fishermen who troll the lake's crystalline waters for their share of the plentiful rainbows (the lake is stocked with 450,000 fingerlings annually). The lake's name comes from the abundance of glassy volcanic rock that litters this region of Umpqua National Forest.

Great fishing notwithstanding, Diamond Lake's popularity can be attributed to a number of other factors. For starters, Diamond Lake is one of the largest natural lakes in Oregon. Add to this its proximity to some spectacular mountain scenery. Follow that up with blissfully warm, dry summer weather. The place is also a convenient distance north of Crater Lake National Park (where frightening numbers of visitors gather in any given summer) and quickly absorbs the overflow. Last but not least, the drive from Roseburg off I-5 follows the pristine and picturesque North Umpqua River most of the way to Diamond Lake on SR 138. This stretch of highway has been called one of the prettiest drives in western America in the summertime, and it is also one of the main connectors between western and eastern Oregon. All of these factors add up to plenty of people most of the time.

The Diamond Lake area is one of those fantastic natural playgrounds that can turn the most resolute vacation planner into a miserable heap of indecision. So many wonderful places. So little time.

> *The lone campground on the western shore of Diamond Lake with views galore and a multitude of recreational options.*

RATINGS

Beauty: ☆ ☆ ☆ ☆ ☆
Privacy: ☆ ☆ ☆ ☆
Spaciousness: ☆ ☆ ☆ ☆ ☆
Quiet: ☆ ☆ ☆ ☆ ☆
Security: ☆ ☆ ☆ ☆
Cleanliness: ☆ ☆ ☆ ☆ ☆
Insect control: ☆ ☆ ☆

KEY INFORMATION

ADDRESS: Timpanogas
Campground
c/o Middle Fork
Ranger District
60 South Pioneer
Street

OPERATED BY: Willamette National
Forest

INFORMATION: (541) 937-2129

OPEN: July to October,
depending on snow
level

SITES: 10

EACH SITE HAS: Picnic table, fire grill

ASSIGNMENT: First come, first
served; no reserva-
tions

REGISTRATION: Self-registration on
site

FACILITIES: Vault toilets, piped
water, garbage ser-
vice

PARKING: At campsites

FEE: $8; $4 per additional
vehicle

ELEVATION: 5,200 feet

RESTRICTIONS: Pets: On leash only
Fires: In fire grills
only
Alcohol: Permitted
Vehicles: 24-foot RV
size limit, no
hookups
Other: 14-day stay
limit

A sizable share of the wonder at Diamond Lake comes in the form of snowy, knife-like mountain peaks—Mount Bailey to the west and, as the campground name implies, Mount Thielsen to the east. Both will take some time to explore, since the only way to fully appreciate them is by foot over arduous trails full of loose, crumbling pumice. The rock is modern-day evidence of the eruption of Mount Mazama some 6,700 years ago.

The upper portion of 9,182-foot Mount Thielsen is a technical climb and should be attempted only by those with the appropriate skills and equipment. Less difficult hikes abound, however, throughout Umpqua National Forest, Mount Thielsen Wilderness, and Oregon Cascades Recreation Area, all within access of Thielsen View Campground. Mount Thielsen Wilderness alone has roughly 125 miles of hiking trails, including a 30-mile section of the Pacific Crest National Scenic Trail. Easier trails in the region range from the 3.2-mile ramble to Horse and Teal Lakes (accessed from the South Shore picnic area) to the longer but still gentle Rodney Butte Trail (6.4 miles roundtrip). A bit steeper challenge awaits on the Tipsoo Trail, which switchbacks for an elevation gain of 1,500 feet to a spectacular vista, and the Howlock Mountain Trail, which is difficult but connects to the Pacific Crest Trail after 7 miles.

Hiking, however, doesn't become an option at the higher elevations much before June, when the heavy snowfalls of winter melt from the trails. In the meantime and at various times throughout the year, there's mountain biking along Forest Service roads and designated trails (except in wilderness areas). For a full-circle look at the area and to get warmed up to more strenuous activity, try the paved bike paths that circle Diamond Lake. Other options are angling in nearby creeks, hunting, birdwatching, canoeing and kayaking the North Umpqua River, and lowland walks to Lemolo Falls and Toketee Falls. If nothing else, there's sitting in camp and enjoying the incredibly clear mountain air.

The approach of winter doesn't slow down activity much in the Diamond Lake area. Although the

MAP

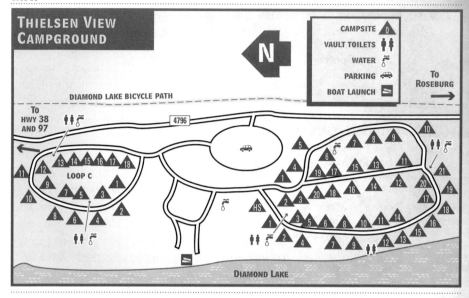

campground is closed, the resort on the east shore of the lake is the focal point for a myriad of skiing and snowmobiling options. At Mount Bailey, you can get in a half-dozen exhilarating runs on pristine powder (considered the best in the state) via a privately run snowcat system. There's a Nordic ski center at Diamond Lake Resort complete with rentals and groomed trails. For the snowmobiler there is a plethora of trails, short or long, guided or on your own. You can ride as far Crater Lake to the south or Crescent Lake to the north (the latter a full-day roundtrip of eight hours).

GETTING THERE

From Roseburg and I-5, take SR 138 to Clearwater (about 50 miles southeast), where the road leaves the North Umpqua and parallels Clearwater River. Turn right onto FS 4795 (Diamond Lake Loop) and head around the north end of Diamond Lake 3.3 miles to Thielsen View Campground on the left. From Medford, take US 62 north to SR 230 north, then continue to SR 138. At FS 4795, turn left and proceed as above. From Klamath Falls or Bend, take US 97 and follow the signs to Diamond Lake Recreation Area.

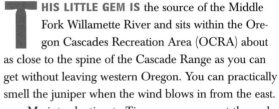

Oakridge

TIMPANOGAS CAMPGROUND

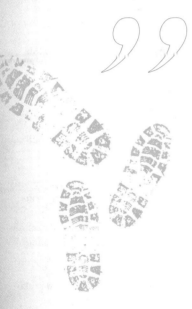

> *An exquisite tent-camping setting on the spine of the Cascades with hiking options in all directions.*

THIS LITTLE GEM IS the source of the Middle Fork Willamette River and sits within the Oregon Cascades Recreation Area (OCRA) about as close to the spine of the Cascade Range as you can get without leaving western Oregon. You can practically smell the juniper when the wind blows in from the east.

My introduction to Timpanogas came at the end of a long, hot day over rough roads and with a fair amount of backtracking—hazards of the job, I'm afraid—but my nerves were shot and my patience was rice-paper thin. Maybe it was this fragile combination, but when I crested the knoll that gave me my first glimpse of Timpanogas Lake and the campground, I wept. Honest! If they had been auctioning off building sites around the lake right then and there, I would have sold body and soul.

After spending weeks on the research trail and developing a keen snobbery for tent camping, I could quickly recognize a keeper when I saw one. First of all, they're so damned rare. And, secondly, you usually find them when you least expect it. Pleasant surprises are still shocking, you know.

I made a fast run through the campground loop, then parked near site 1. I was in a daze for about the first 15 minutes as I digested the exquisite setting that lay before me. I almost didn't want to move for fear it would disappear in a poof!

Let me describe the scene, and you can make your own assessment: The faint but distinctive chirping of an eagle carried across the water from its perch high in the forest of firs bordering the lake. A bright red canoe slid into view from the periphery of the lake, contrasting pleasantly with the deep blue water and the rich green forest. A bold chipmunk scratched around nervously under the picnic table, hoping I had brought new and interesting forage. Songbirds flitted

RATINGS

Beauty: ✿ ✿ ✿
Privacy: ✿ ✿ ✿ ✿
Spaciousness: ✿ ✿ ✿ ✿
Quiet: ✿ ✿ ✿ ✿ ✿
Security: ✿ ✿ ✿
Cleanliness: ✿ ✿ ✿
Insect control: ✿ ✿ ✿

everywhere. Waterfowl bobbed along the water's edge. The fragrance of an early evening campfire mixed with the warm mountain scents of a late afternoon sun.

How are we doing so far? Idyllic, you say? Absolutely. This is prototypical Timpanogas, and I hope it never changes. You know what they say. First impressions are lasting.

The campground itself is an elegantly simplistic collection of sites, all but two of which claim "low-bank waterfront" and "private moorage" in their brochure descriptions. The two vanguards (sites 1 and 7) can at least claim "territorial views" of the lake or the surrounding campground. There isn't one site that doesn't have what real-estate agents call curb appeal. Each sits on practically a full-sized city lot and if you get to "own" site 9 for a few days, you'll have the best claim to pumped-water rights.

Conversely, site 5 sits at an awkward distance from the water spigot on the spur road to the Timpanogas Basin trailhead. Not to be outdone, however, it features the most shaded setting under a high crown of varietal firs. Thick underbrush otherwise maintains maximum privacy between sites along the camp road and tree cover is just enough to allow for filtered sun in some places, direct blasts in others. The sites are so spaciously distant from each other, however, that lack of privacy is hardly a consideration. It's the kind of community—intimate as it may seem—where you can choose to meet your neighbors or not.

Maybe it's the high altitude (5,200 feet) and the achingly fresh air that energizes your sense of discovery at Timpanogas. Maybe it's the ghostly presence of pioneers who stalwartly clambered with their cumbersome wagons and ox teams over the Cascades at nearby Emigrant Pass. Maybe it's the call of the Pacific Crest National Scenic Trail, which passes only a few miles east.

Whatever the inspiration, a restlessness sets in at Timpanogas once the initial shock of such a pleasant place has passed. More than 25 trail miles connect within the Timpanogas Basin alone, leading to such

KEY INFORMATION

ADDRESS:	Timpanogas Lake Campground c/o Middle Fork Ranger District 60 South Pioneer Street Lowell, OR 97413
OPERATED BY:	Willamette National Forest
INFORMATION:	(541) 937-2129
OPEN:	July to October, depending on snow level
SITES:	10
EACH SITE HAS:	Picnic table, fire grill; some shade trees
ASSIGNMENT:	First come, first served; no reservations
REGISTRATION:	Self-registration on site
FACILITIES:	Pit toilets, piped water, garbage service
PARKING:	At campsites
FEE:	$8, $4 per additional vehicle
ELEVATION:	5,200 feet
RESTRICTIONS:	Pets: On leash only Fires: In fire pits only Alcohol: Permitted Vehicles: 24-foot RV size limit, no hookups Other: 14-day stay limit

MAP

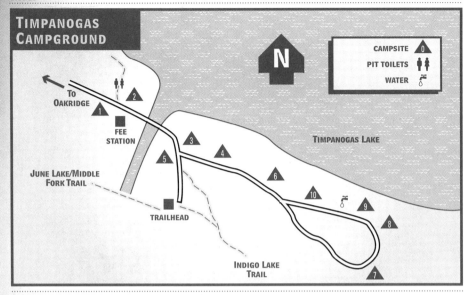

TIMPANOGAS CAMPGROUND

N

CAMPSITE 0
PIT TOILETS
WATER

TO OAKRIDGE

FEE STATION

TIMPANOGAS LAKE

JUNE LAKE/MIDDLE FORK TRAIL

TRAILHEAD

INDIGO LAKE TRAIL

GETTING THERE

Timpanogas Lake is 43 miles southeast of Oakridge by way of the following route: From OR 58 2 miles east of Oakridge, take Kitson Springs Road (FS 23) south briefly to its intersection with FS 21 (alternately known in spots as Rigdon Road and Military Road). Turn right on FS 21, passing Hills Creek Reservoir and numerous campgrounds—including Sacandaga—and along the Middle Fork Willamette River for roughly 32 miles to FS 2154. Turn left and follow the road for 10 miles to the campground. Stretches of FS 2154 are rough and steep, as the elevation gain is rapid as you approach 5,200 feet.

delights as Opal Lake, Indigo Lake (with a hike-in campsite), June Lake, and politically incorrect Amos and Andy Lakes. Views in all directions are possible from certain trail vantage points, with Sawtooth Mountain to the south, Cowhorn Mountain (at 7,664 feet, the highest point in the OCRA) to the east, and Diamond Peak to the north. The same Middle Fork Willamette River Trail that passes by Sacandaga Campground (see page 119) ends at Timpanogas Lake and is a 25-mile one-way trek along the river's banks and parts of the Central Military Wagon Road.

Wintertime activities in the OCRA are gaining in popularity, namely snowmobiling (since the recreation designation allows for semi-primitive motorized use) and cross-country skiing.

EASTERN OREGON

ANTHONY LAKES CAMPGROUND

ANTHONY LAKES CAMPGROUND, at 7,100-foot elevation and only 30 miles northwest of Baker City, is part of the Anthony Lakes Recreation Area, which also includes the much smaller and less developed Mud Lake Campground (with only six sites) and the Anthony Lakes Day-Use Area, popular with valley dwellers seeking a high-altitude escape from the heat far below.

The view from just about any campsite at Anthony Lakes is simply picture-perfect, with the shimmering blue of Anthony Lake contrasting against the dark, subalpine forest greens and the rocky, rugged flanks of surrounding Elkhorn Mountains. At this altitude, the fragrances of high-mountain eastern Oregon are irresistible, with pungent notes of woods, earth, and water mingling in the rarefied air. Find one of the sun-warmed, smooth rocks edging the lake, maybe an overhanging tree for a little shade, then dangle a toe or two in the cool waters and indulge yourself.

Unfortunately, if it's a normal summer, the mosquitoes may have you on the go in no time. It's the curse of such a beautiful setting with such a short summer season. They weren't particularly bad in the summer of 2003, but then it wasn't a normal summer, as the snow melt was long gone by mid-July. Winter recreationists are in luck, since they can enjoy the same views mosquito-free at the Anthony Lakes Ski Area right next door and also some of the best powder in Oregon at the highest ski base in the state. Food for thought if you're so inclined and getting eaten alive.

Campsites come in a variety of options if you arrive early. Despite its out-of-the-way feel, this spot does get busy on summer weekends. The main camping area, configured in two loops, sits above and away from the lake as you drive in off FS 73 (Elkhorn Scenic

> *If there's a higher campground in Oregon that has a paved road right to its front door, I'd love to know about it!*

RATINGS

Beauty: ☆ ☆ ☆
Privacy: ☆ ☆ ☆ ☆
Spaciousness: ☆ ☆ ☆ ☆
Quiet: ☆ ☆ ☆ ☆
Security: ☆ ☆ ☆ ☆ ☆
Cleanliness: ☆ ☆ ☆ ☆
Insect control: ☆ ☆

Drive). These are sites 1–27, and I have to say they would not be my first choice. Very tightly spaced, these sites have decent vegetation groundcover, but privacy is at a premium. Try for one that sits on the outside of the loop for the least-crowded feel.

I found the best sites to be the walk-ins (28–32), which are in optimum proximity to lake views, gener-ously spaced, and close enough to parking for easy unloading of gear and provisions. They are, however, staggered on either side of the footpath that circum-navigates the lake, which may get busy when other campers are out for a shoreside stroll.

A string of campsites, numbered 33–39, lies on the far south side of the lake beyond the boat launch. These sites are spaced similarly to the walk-in sites, but being on the flats and closer to the lake may enhance the mosquito presence. They are also closer to the boat put-in, which could mean early morning noise.

Nearby are the original Civilian Conservation Corps campsites, preserved from 1933 when workers were busy getting the ski area ready for opening. It was one of the first in the country and at the time totally modern thanks to the newest invention of the day: the rope tow.

Activities abound in the Anthony Lakes area year-round. South and west of the campground is the Baldy Unit of the North Fork John Day Wilderness, a small, rugged area with hiking options in uncrowded terrain. Access to the Elkhorn Range contained within parts of the wilderness is available via the Elkhorn National Scenic Trail, which departs very near Anthony Lakes. Peaks and buttes in the Elkhorns rise as high as 9,100 feet, offering magnificent vistas of this compact but diverse pocket of the Blue Mountains.

You're likely to see as much wildlife as people; the region supports herds of elk and various deer species, black bear, mountain lions, mountain goats, hawks, and the occasional (seasonal) bald eagle. Conse-quently, however, it's a popular hunting area in the fall. The North Fork John Day River, designated wild and scenic in one stretch west of Anthony Lakes, is known for its abundant fish populations, including chi-nook and steelhead migrating in astounding numbers

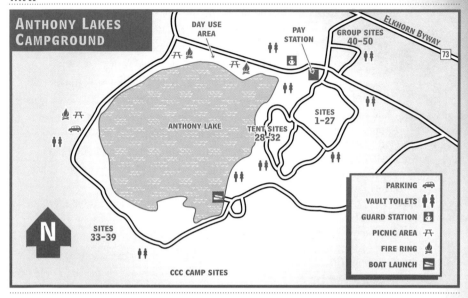

ANTHONY LAKES CAMPGROUND

DAY USE AREA

PAY STATION

GROUP SITES 40–50

ELKHORN BYWAY

73

ANTHONY LAKE

TENT SITES 28–32

SITES 1–27

N

SITES 33–39

CCC CAMP SITES

PARKING	🚐
VAULT TOILETS	👫
GUARD STATION	🏠
PICNIC AREA	🏕
FIRE RING	🔥
BOAT LAUNCH	⛵

up from the Columbia. Brook trout, Dolly Vardens, and rainbows also thrive in the North Fork.

Historically speaking, more people frequented this area on a regular basis around the turn of the century than do today. The discovery of gold in the late 1860s combined with a flourishing lumber industry, pioneer ranching, and completion of the transcontinental railroad contributed to a healthy stretch of boom years for towns such as Granite, Sumpter, Austin, and Bourne. Though much has been destroyed by time, fire, and neglect, there are a few buildings scattered throughout the region still standing as tribute to that rough-and-tumble period in Oregon history.

One of the best ways to gain a richer appreciation of the area is to drive the entire Elkhorn National Scenic loop—a 106-mile paved route with marked points of interest along the way. It's a good day-tripping option if you make Anthony Lakes Campground your base.

GETTING THERE

Anthony Lakes is 30 miles northwest of Baker City following US 30 to CR 1146 to FS 73. Follow signs directing you to Anthony Lakes Ski Area or along the Elkhorn Scenic Byway when in doubt.

BUCKHORN CAMPGROUND

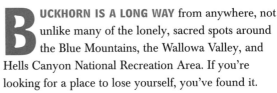

> *When one ranger tells you about a secret place, you figure it's worth a look. When two rangers tell you about the spot, you know you've got a keeper.*

BUCKHORN IS A LONG WAY from anywhere, not unlike many of the lonely, sacred spots around the Blue Mountains, the Wallowa Valley, and Hells Canyon National Recreation Area. If you're looking for a place to lose yourself, you've found it.

The campground itself is not the centerpiece of the Buckhorn experience; it is simply the place to pitch your tent, come back to in the evening, tell stories over the crackling campfire, and rub your sore feet after the day of hot, dusty trailblazing to which you've willingly subjected yourself. Okay, so you're not exactly the first person who's been out here (or there wouldn't even be this primitive campground), but at Buckhorn you get the feeling that you could be the last person to visit for a long time.

The sense of loneliness begins on the drive up from Enterprise, when you start out on the Crow Creek Road off of OR 82. At indistinctly marked junctions, the road becomes Zumwalt-Imnaha Road, then Zumwalt-Buckhorn Road, then FS 46. There's no one on the road to ask for directions; ranch houses are tucked deep in the folding fields and usually have gated entrances.

All of these anxieties aside, the Zumwalt ranks as a modern-day magic carpet ride. Miles and miles of burnished gold and brown grasslands roll out before you as you climb gently but steadily on a gravel expressway through this magnificent benchland, the smooth contours and rich colors contrasting sharply with the stark, contorted shadowy jumble of the canyons to the east and the jagged, snowcapped peaks of the Wallowas in the rear-view mirror.

The few campsites (five total) that comprise Buckhorn are heavily vegetated (which is a pleasant surprise given the otherwise sparsely shrubbed ground). This is due, in large part, to the presence of Buckhorn Spring, a stalwart little underground spurt that creates an oasis

RATINGS

Beauty: ☆ ☆ ☆
Privacy: ☆ ☆ ☆ ☆ ☆
Spaciousness: ☆ ☆ ☆ ☆
Quiet: ☆ ☆ ☆ ☆ ☆
Security: ☆
Cleanliness: ☆ ☆
Insect control: ☆ ☆ ☆ ☆

of plantlife in this harsh environment. When you drop down to the campground on FS 783 from the main access road (FS 780), which continues on to the lookout, you will feel as though you've stumbled onto a private thicket that could easily be an afternoon resting ground for local deer.

Quickly assessing that primitive is a generous word for Buckhorn Campground, you will also recognize that the beauty of this campground lies in its remoteness, its raw simplicity, and its location a mere hundred yards from the mesmerizing view. The familiar "less is more" attitude is a good one to adopt when taking in the wonders from this perch on Oregon's northeastern rim.

Here, you actually get two views for the price of one, as Buckhorn sits high above the lower Imnaha River near where it empties into the mighty Snake. Flashes of brilliant sunlight on the river far below catch your eye. Raptors soar in the thermal currents high above. At eye level as far as you can see, ridges and tables and knobs and shelves of varying geophysical proportions and timelines thrust and jut and hunker and lean in an incomparable tableau. It's panorama-plus through a viewfinder, and in all honesty, I've never seen a photograph that did it justice.

It's easy to see why Chief Joseph and his peaceful band of Nez Perce so loved this land—and why the U.S. government wanted control of it, too. Exploitation and misunderstandings ensued, and Chief Joseph was forced out. The Nee-Mee-Poo (meaning "the real people") Trail, which follows part of the Imnaha to a crossing at the Snake River, marks the displaced tribe's exodus on its long, tormented trek eastward through Idaho and Montana. The Nee-Mee-Poo is not far from Buckhorn, as the crow flies, but too far for a day hike in the area's hot, dry, steep conditions. A recommended alternative is the hike to Spain Saddle for continuously impressive views of the Imnaha and Snake River Canyons and even the Salmon River deeper into Idaho.

ADDRESS: Buckhorn Campground c/o Wallowa Valley Ranger District 88401 Oregon Highway 82 Enterprise, OR 97828

OPERATED BY: Wallowa-Whitman National Forest

INFORMATION: (541) 426-4978

OPEN: May to late September

SITES: 5

EACH SITE HAS: Picnic table, shade trees; four with fire grills

ASSIGNMENT: First come, first served; no reservations

REGISTRATION: Not necessary

FACILITIES: Pit toilet; no piped water

PARKING: At campsites

FEE: None

ELEVATION: 5,200 feet

RESTRICTIONS: Pets: On leash only
Fires: In fire pits only
Alcohol: Permitted
Vehicles: Not recommended for RVs

MAP

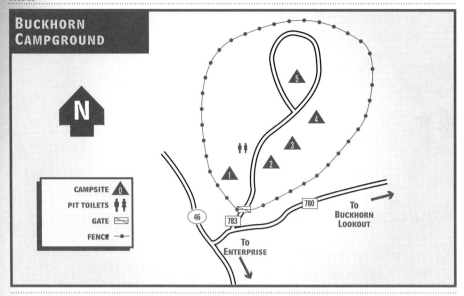

BUCKHORN CAMPGROUND

N

CAMPSITE	0
PIT TOILETS	♀♂
GATE	⊠
FENCE	●—●—

46   783   780

To ENTERPRISE

To BUCKHORN LOOKOUT

GETTING THERE

Buckhorn is 43 miles north-east of Enterprise (which is east of LaGrande on OR 82). From OR 82, take the Crow Creek Road to Zumwalt Road. Turn right and continue to FS 46, then turn right again on FS 780. The roads out here aren't particularly well-marked. I had to stop several times to make sure I was taking the correct fork. A good local road map wouldn't be a bad idea. Nearly the entire drive is on fine gravel, so expect a dust cloud following you like a posse in the summer.

Enjoy Buckhorn for what it was then, is today, and mostly, for what it isn't. Take away an appreciation of some of the most wild, untamed areas of Oregon desperately trying to remain that way, and when it comes time to vote to preserve this special place, do the right thing.

DAIRY POINT CAMPGROUND

Paisley

DAIRY POINT CAMPGROUND IS the kind of place where you wouldn't be surprised to see Gary Cooper splashing across Dairy Creek on his trusty steed, clomping up to your tent site, and saying in his quiet way, "Howdy, folks. Mind if I share your campfire tonight?"

This is classic western territory that is long on the drive getting there (unless you live in Lakeview or Klamath Falls), short on the crowds, and big on the amount of territory to explore, whether Gary Cooper offers to be your guide or not.

The campground is miniscule compared to most listings in this book and is quite primitive. Nevertheless, it qualifies for inclusion on the beauty factor though it falls short elsewhere and it does have piped water, which is often not the case at less-developed locations. The Fremont National Forest Web site says that Dairy Point is full on most holidays and summer weekends—and they put that in capital letters. Frankly, I find it hard to believe, but there must be a devoted following that draws from the modest populations down there in Lakeview and Klamath Falls. If you're coming from any of the metropolitan centers on the west side of the Cascades, it's easily a full day getting here and another getting back. Since Dairy Point operates on a first come, first serve basis, it would be a good idea to have a Plan B.

Given the campground's popularity and site limitations, I'm surprised the Forest Service hasn't found the funds to create a few more campsites, which could blend harmoniously into the creekside and not spoil the natural surroundings. I saw a giant RV taking up half the main meadow area when I was there, trampling down a wide swath of grasses and wildflowers in order to park its rear end under a shade tree. I could easily envision several tent sites in place of the hulking RV,

> *The backdrop is classic Western, and Dairy Creek provides a lush setting for a primitive escape.*

RATINGS

Beauty: ✿ ✿ ✿ ✿ ✿
Privacy: ✿ ✿ ✿
Spaciousness: ✿ ✿ ✿ ✿ ✿
Quiet: ✿ ✿ ✿ ✿
Security: ✿ ✿
Cleanliness: ✿ ✿ ✿
Insect control: ✿ ✿ ✿

KEY INFORMATION

ADDRESS: Dairy Point
Campground
c/o Paisley Ranger
District
Oregon Highway 31
or P.O. Box 67
Paisley, OR 97636

OPERATED BY: Fremont-Winema
National Forests

INFORMATION: (541) 943-3114

OPEN: Mid-May through
October

SITES: 4

EACH SITE HAS: Picnic table, fire
grill; some shade
trees

ASSIGNMENT: First come, first
served; no reserva-
tions

REGISTRATION: Not necessary

FACILITIES: Vault toilets, hand-
pumped water, pic-
nic area, horseshoe
pits

PARKING: At campsites

FEE: None

ELEVATION: 5,200 feet

RESTRICTIONS: Pets: On leash only
Fires: In fire pits
only
Alcohol: Permitted
Vehicles: 21-foot RV
size limit, no
hookups

and since there's no fee at Dairy Point, it's not as if the RVs bring in more money. Okay, there's my two cents.

The campsites—all four of them—sit on the edge of Dairy Creek where a buffer of beautiful lush grasses lines the shores. Small sand bars have formed along the creek with tufts of grass occasionally claiming this territory, too. White fir and ponderosa pine provide the canopy overhead, and tall mountains ring the wide valley as Dairy Creek meanders around the base of Buck Mountain to meet up with the Chewaucan River.

This is a prime rainbow trout stream, coming fresh and clear off the flanks of Gearhart Mountain with deep, cool pools curling around the sand bars to provide shady relief for unsuspecting trout. I visited late in a bone-dry summer, and I was pleasantly surprised to see Dairy Creek with a generous flow when other creekbeds further west and north were painfully low.

For recreation, the landscape makes you want to head for the nearest horse stable and venture out into the hills, just as John Fremont did when he first traveled in this area in the mid 1840s. There are a few equestrian outfitters in Lakeview if this suits your fancy. For those who want to explore by foot, the Gearhart Mountain Wilderness, west of Dairy Point along FS 34, is just the right size, with only 15 miles of trails but quite a diverse terrain. The Gearhart Wilderness came under protection way back in 1964 with the original Wilderness Act. Additional lands were added 20 years later and it remains today at 22,809 acres (small by comparison to most protected lands in Oregon). From the top of Gearhart Mountain (elevation 8,364 feet), one can view the peaks of Central Oregon to the north, Mount Lassen in California to the south, and Steens Mountain in Oregon's Outback to the east.

There are a number of ways to find Dairy Point. I came at it from FS 28 out of Silver Lake, thinking I was taking a shortcut. Rising and falling with the contours of the topography, I worked my way past shrouded marshlands, through spacious meadow clearings, and between dense stands of pine, fir, spruce, and juniper; I saw only one car for three hours—and it was parked in a meadow where the owner trained his bird-hunting dog. Three-plus hours later, I turned the final

MAP

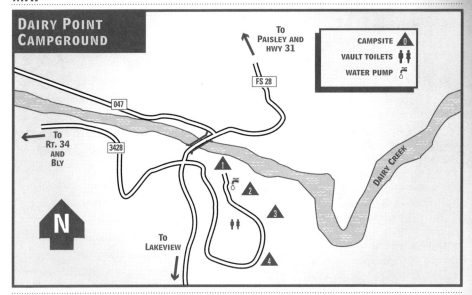

DAIRY POINT CAMPGROUND

To PAISLEY AND HWY 31

CAMPSITE

VAULT TOILETS

WATER PUMP

FS 28

047

To RT. 34 AND BLY

3428

1

2

3

4

N

To LAKEVIEW

DAIRY CREEK

corner at the juncture with FS 47 and crossed the bridge to Dairy Point. If you have the time, FS 28 is a remarkable find.

The more obvious route is the drive between Paisley and LaPine (south of Bend) on OR 31. This stretch of highway is breathtaking in any season, as the route takes in the astounding endlessness of the Summer Lake basin. Under the right conditions at the right time of day, a Summer Lake sunset can wash across the enormous sky in shades of fuchsia, raspberry, crimson, mandarin orange, eggplant, and cotton-candy pink. It takes an amazingly long time for the colors to subside, which is good news for us picture-takers scrambling for the camera and a place to pull the car over.

GETTING THERE

From OR 31 in Paisley (north of Lakeview), take Mill Street to the Y junction and stay left to continue on FS 33 for 20 miles. This road meets FS 28 at a T where you will turn left. Follow FS 28 for just over 2 miles, crossing Dairy Creek Bridge. The campground is to the immediate left over the bridge.

HIDDEN CAMPGROUND

> *After the long, hot, dusty, and circuitous drive to Hidden Campground (either way you come, it's all that and slightly confusing, too), you'll just have one thing to say: "Ahhh . . ."*

A PEACEFUL, BEAUTIFUL, almost poetic setting on the shoulders of the upper Imnaha River, it's even easier to appreciate Hidden Campground after the drive down from Joseph, which I found to be a real test. What starts off as a gentle grade up on Little Sheep Creek Road, with wide views of the Wallowa Valley as it falls away behind you, quickly becomes a twisting, narrow, roller-coaster ride when you turn right onto FS 39 (Wallowa Mountain Loop Road).

Keeping both hands on the wheel is vital as you pass through an extensively burned area and work your way towards the ultimate drop down to the Imnaha River Road, approximately 30 miles from the start of Wallowa Mountain Loop Road. I found the road signs confusing even with a good USGS map. Although the road following the Imnaha both north and south is officially the Imnaha River Road, to the left it is FS 3955 and to the right it continues briefly as FS 39 and then becomes FS 3960. At this intersection, the main road, FS 39, takes an angle left towards its intersection with OR 86. The key is to keep taking rights—never a left—and you will ultimately find your way to Hidden Campground. Perhaps others had similar problems locating the campground and named it accordingly.

The campground itself is not hidden at all. In fact, it is one of the few campgrounds along the Imnaha that offers gorgeous, open sites with lovely tall grasses under towering ponderosa pines and tamarack. Sun filters through the tall trees and a cooling breeze kicks off the fast-falling Imnaha to make for a heavenly combination on a scorching summer day.

Granted, Hidden Campground is about as primitive as they come, with only a picnic table and fire grill at each of its ten sites. Every site sits well-spaced from its neighbors along the river, so there's no chance of a

RATINGS

Beauty: ✪ ✪ ✪ ✪ ✪
Privacy: ✪ ✪ ✪ ✪
Spaciousness: ✪ ✪ ✪ ✪ ✪
Quiet: ✪ ✪ ✪ ✪ ✪
Security: ✪ ✪ ✪
Cleanliness: ✪ ✪ ✪ ✪
Insect control: ✪ ✪ ✪ ✪

particularly bad spot despite sparse ground cover. Sites 8, 9, and 10 are located on the loop where outgoing traffic circles by, and may experience a bit more noise as a result. The wind in the trees and the sounds of the river ought to drown out most disturbances, which would be temporary anyway. The Forest Service rates Hidden as a high-use facility, but when I was there in midsummer midweek, there were only two sites taken. Blessedly, there were no RVs, which glutted the more developed campgrounds that I passed on the way in.

Aside from an overkill of four outhouses, there's very little else that interrupts the natural environment at Hidden. And this is as it should be, since the campground is located within the Hells Canyon National Recreation Area and surrounded by just about every wilderness, wild and scenic, and national forest boundary possible. Immediately west, the officially designated Wild and Scenic segment of the Imnaha River plunges out of the Wallowa Mountains. A little further west is the boundary for the Eagle Cap Wilderness and the only trail access into it from this side of the Wallowas (from Indian Crossing Campground at road's end). Due east is Hells Canyon Wilderness and the Wild and Scenic Snake River. Beyond that, there's Idaho. This is the southeasternmost boundary of the Wallowa National Forest, and just across the river on the Imnaha's south bank is the northeasternmost corner of the Whitman National Forest.

If you need any guidance on things to do, a hike into the Eagle Cap Wilderness is number one on my list. Next are the Imnaha River Trail and the Imnaha Crossing Trail. Afterwards, make the drive to McGraw Lookout for an unstoppable view over Hells Canyon and some well-placed interpretive plaques and meditation benches. The drive north along the Imnaha River Road leads you to other Hells Canyon overlook points and to the town of Imnaha.

Traveling south along FS 39 and onto OR 86 to the west, the route of the Wallow Mountain Loop Road continues. This is more than a one-day loop from your starting point at Hidden (unless you get a really early start), so you may want to retrace your steps at about Halfway (the name of the town, not the mileage mark)

KEY INFORMATION

ADDRESS: Hidden Campground c/o Wallowa Valley Ranger District 88401 Oregon Highway 82 Enterprise, OR | 97828

OPERATED BY: Wallowa-Whitman National Forest

INFORMATION: (541) 426-4978

OPEN: Mid-April to mid-October

SITES: 10

EACH SITE HAS: Picnic table, fire grill; some shade trees

ASSIGNMENT: First come, first served; no reservation

REGISTRATION: Self-registration on site

FACILITIES: Vault toilets, no piped water

PARKING: At campsites

FEE: $5

ELEVATION: 4,400 feet

RESTRICTIONS: Pets: On leash only Fires: In fire grills only Alcohol: Permitted Vehicles: Small RVs or trailers okay, no hookups

MAP

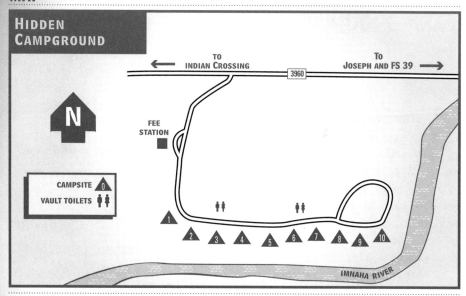

HIDDEN CAMPGROUND

TO INDIAN CROSSING ← | 3960 | → To JOSEPH AND FS 39

N

FEE STATION ■

CAMPSITE ▲ 0
VAULT TOILETS 👫

IMNAHA RIVER

GETTING THERE

From Joseph, take SR 350 (Little Sheep Creek Highway) to FS 39 (Wallowa Mountain Loop). At the intersection with the Imnaha River Road (FS 3960), turn right and follow the river to Hidden's entrance on your left. You'll pass several other campgrounds on the Imnaha Road. The driving distance from Joseph is roughly 44 miles; the last 9 are gravel and everything in between is steep, narrow, and twisting. It's very slow going. The lower Imnaha is home to a daunting system of Forest Service roads that all seem to look alike. A good local road map is a must.

or take OR 86 east to the town of Copperfield for a different perspective of Hells Canyon and a look at Oxbow Dam.

Paddlers are advised that the Imnaha River in the vicinity of Hidden requires expert skills, and even then it may be a foolhardy venture. The river drops very steeply and is log- and debris-choked in many spots, demanding a thorough scouting of the waters before any descents are considered. The buddy system is essential in this technical, remote area.

JUBILEE LAKE CAMPGROUND

Tollgate

ALTHOUGH THIS IS THE LARGEST (only 50 sites, though) and most popular campground in the Umatilla National Forest (pronounced "YOU-ma-TIL-lah"), you still may be able to get some elbow room here, as the 1.4-million acre national forest is renowned for its rustic and remote wilderness. Native Americans named the area Umatilla, which means "water rippling over sands," and water still trickles down wooded slopes to chilly Jubilee Lake.

One reason Jubilee Lake Campground is so popular is that there's plenty to do right in the campground itself. The lake is a hot spot for fishing, where people bring their boats or perch themselves in one of the many private waterside nooks. The 2.8-mile, forested Jubilee Lake National Recreation Area Trail winds around the peaceful lake, with benches placed conveniently so you can soak in the scenery. Like most campground facilities, it is wheelchair-accessible.

The area is renowned among bird-watchers, who gaze across the lake through field glasses hoping to spot three-toed woodpeckers, mountain bluebirds, and western tanagers. Approximately 214 species of birds have been documented in Umatilla National Forest. According to park literature, the northern half of the forest above I-84 is wetter and is home to many birds commonly found in the Rocky Mountains. The southern half of the forest below I-84 is dryer and flatter, home to bird species more commonly seen in the Great Basin.

For those who crave a little more action and adventure, there are plenty of nearby trails that are not nearly as crowded, unless you count the deer and rattlesnakes (keep your eyes open!). In particular, several neighboring trails take you down the steep canyons into the South Fork Walla Walla River—great if you prefer to skip the lakeside route and add a real work-

> *Jubilee Lake is a popular area for anglers and birders in the rugged and remote Umatilla National Forest.*

RATINGS

Beauty: ✿ ✿ ✿ ✿
Privacy: ✿ ✿
Spaciousness: ✿ ✿ ✿
Quiet: ✿ ✿
Security: ✿ ✿ ✿
Cleanliness: ✿ ✿
Insect Control: ✿ ✿ ✿

ADDRESS: Jubilee Lake
Campground
c/o Walla Walla
Ranger District
1415 West Rose
Walla Walla, WA
99362

OPERATED BY: Umatilla National
Forest

INFORMATION: (509) 522-6290

OPEN: Mid-June through
September

SITES: 52

EACH SITE HAS: Picnic table, fire ring

ASSIGNMENT: First come,
first serve; no
reservations

REGISTRATION: Self-registration at
campground
entrance

FACILITIES: Vault toilets, piped
water, firewood

PARKING: At campsites or at
day-use area

FEE: $14; $5 per additional vehicle; $3
entry fee at day-use
area

ELEVATION: 4,800 feet

RESTRICTIONS: Pets: On leash only
Fires: In fire rings
only
Alcohol: Permitted
Vehicles: One car
per site parking

out to your day. If you come across people wandering in the forest, don't worry, they're not lost: Huckleberry and morel mushroom picking is a popular activity in the area during summer months.

Huckleberry season runs from late summer through early fall. Many berry hunters frequent "secret" berry stashes that perhaps only they and a few Native Americans from ages past have sampled. To find the best berries, native peoples used to follow bears, who supposedly have a pretty good nose for finding the sweetest fruit. Huckleberries resemble blue-berries, but have a thicker skin and contain tiny crunchy seeds that ere edible. Blueberries are sweeter in general, but huckleberries may be substituted in most any recipe that calls for blueberries. The best way to gather the berries is to spread a cloth on the ground beneath the bush. Shake the bush and the cloth will catch the ripe fruit.

Located at a cool altitude of 4,800 feet, the camp-ground closes in winter, but Jubilee Lake is neverthe-less a popular destination for snowmobile riders, who can follow Jubilee Lake Trail (FS 64) from the tollgate to the lake. Skyline Trail (FS 6403) connects with Jubilee Lake Trail at Bald Mountain and offers far-reaching views of the Walla Walla Valley and Jubilee Lake. Naturally, these trails are open to foot and bicy-cle traffic in warmer months. They are part of a 200-mile network in the northern half of Umatilla National Forest, so it's wise to consult with the Walla Walla Ranger District before setting out. They can provide route options as well as forest maps.

Although it may tend to get more packed than other area campgrounds, Jubilee Lake Campground is included in this guide because of its natural beauty and lake access; you can easily leave the crowds along the lakeshore. Keep in mind that the entrance road is only open when the snow clears, which is typically not until mid-June, so plan accordingly. Also, since there are only a scattering of small towns in the area, make sure you top off your gas tank before you arrive, because gas stations are few and far between.

MAP

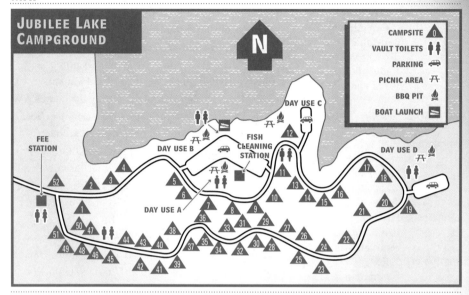

JUBILEE LAKE CAMPGROUND

N

CAMPSITE
VAULT TOILETS
PARKING
PICNIC AREA
BBQ PIT
BOAT LAUNCH

FEE STATION

DAY USE C

DAY USE B

FISH CLEANING STATION

DAY USE D

DAY USE A

GETTING THERE

From Tollgate, turn left onto FS 64. Drive 12 miles on the dirt road, following signs to Jubilee Lake Campground.

MINAM STATE RECREATION AREA CAMPGROUND

> *Minam State Park is a perfect jumping-off point for rafters, anglers, and hikers.*

IF YOU'RE LOOKING FOR a cozy, secluded campsite, look elsewhere: All of the primitive campsites in this campground are in a huge open clearing where you can wave to your neighbors. But don't discount it just yet. What it may lack in privacy, Minam State Recreation Area certainly makes up for in other areas.

For starters, it sits pretty in a remote valley on a steep bank overlooking the whitewater of Wallowa River, which is a popular destination for both rafters and anglers. Large pine trees dominate the landscape.

The Indians called this area—which extends from the mouth of Indian valley where the Grande Ronde narrows, down to the confluence of the Grande Ronde and Wallowa Rivers—"Hunaha." Lochow Lochow, "lovely little forest," was the central Indian camp for the Nez Perce, who harvested wild vegetables, fruit, fish, and game through the summer months.

Two launching points for boaters are located in the nearby day-use area, and you can even rent a raft at the nearby store. Some rafters even return from their runs with tales of bighorn sheep sightings. Anglers will also enjoy this area, as the river is renowned for steelhead and rainbow trout. You can catch your dinner and make use of that fire pit back at your campsite.

Water adventures aren't the only thing drawing visitors; the nearby Wallowa Mountains offer some of the best all-day hiking and backpacking trails in the state, making this a perfect spot to set up camp along the way and return to after a day of hiking. It's also not nearly as crowded as nearby Wallowa Lake Campground—even on a holiday weekend, you're likely to find an empty spot on which to pitch your tent along the steep canyon wall overlooking the river. Keep your eyes open, as the area plays host to

RATINGS

Beauty: ✰ ✰ ✰ ✰
Privacy: ✰ ✰
Spaciousness: ✰ ✰ ✰ ✰
Quiet: ✰ ✰ ✰
Security: ✰ ✰ ✰ ✰
Cleanliness: ✰ ✰ ✰ ✰
Cleanliness: ✰ ✰

wildlife such as bear, elk, and deer. Bear sightings were a common conversation topic on my visit.

While the campsites may seem a little confusing as you first enter the campground—they aren't well-marked upon first glance and there's no clear-cut difference between one site and its neighbor—there are advantages to this open type of campground. For one thing, it's a prime spot if you're bringing a large group along, because your group can camp on the large grassy knolls. Some of the sites offer asphalt tent pads, and most have water nearby. All of the sites offer views of the Wallowa River. A nearby store will stock you up with ice, food, and fishing supplies. But be warned: It tends to close early, so make sure you don't return from an all-day hiking trip with a big thirst, only to be disappointed. It's best to come prepared, but Elgin is only about 10 miles west so you're not completely out of luck.

If you find yourself recovering from the aches of a long hike or rafting trip, Elgin also offers a unique way to view the valley's majestic scenery—by rail. The Eagle Cap Excursion Train (phone (800) 323-7330) offers round-trip rides from nearby Wallowa to Joseph, where you can sit back and enjoy view from the train's Pullman cars. Don't forget to bring your camera.

However you decide to enjoy this natural setting, keep in mind that the climate in Eastern Oregon varies greatly with elevation. The higher up you go, the colder the temperatures and higher the chance of precipitation. If you're visiting the region during the summer months, be prepared for afternoon thunderstorms and chilly evening temperatures. Don't be surprised if you encounter snow on high country trails, at any time of year.

KEY INFORMATION

ADDRESS:	Minam State Recreation Area 72214 Marina Lane Minam, OR 97846
OPERATED BY:	Oregon State Parks
INFORMATION:	(541) 432-8855, (800) 551-6949; www.oregonstateparks.org
OPEN:	April through November
SITES:	12
EACH SITE HAS:	Picnic table, fire ring
ASSIGNMENT:	First-come, first-served; no reservations
REGISTRATION:	Self-registration on site
FACILITIES:	Vault toilets, piped water
PARKING:	At campsites
FEE:	$8 May through September, $5 October through April; $5 per additional vehicle
ELEVATION:	2,500 feet
RESTRICTIONS:	Pets: On leash only Fires: In fire rings only Alcohol: Permitted at campsites only Vehicles: One car per site parking Other: 14-day stay limit

MAP

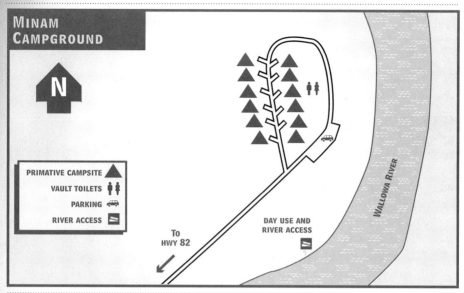

MINAM CAMPGROUND

N

PRIMATIVE CAMPSITE ▲
VAULT TOILETS 👫
PARKING 🚗
RIVER ACCESS

To
HWY 82

DAY USE AND
RIVER ACCESS

WALLOWA RIVER

GETTING THERE

From Elgin, drive 13 miles
northeast on US 82, and turn
left (north) at the sign for
Minam State Recreation
Area. Drive 2 miles to the
end of the road and the
campground.

OLIVE LAKE CAMPGROUND

BEFORE GOING FURTHER, I must first confess that Olive Lake was not initially one of my top 50 campgrounds. Sometimes, the fickle finger of campground-research fate has the last word, and so it was on the day that Olive Lake jumped onto the "A list."

Fortunately, Olive Lake turned out to be a more than adequate alternative. It has played such an integral role throughout the history of this region, from the early gold-mining days to its contemporary recognition as a valuable focal point for area recreation, habitat restoration, and historical preservation. The combination makes for an interesting blend, offering opportunities to learn and explore in one of the least-traveled areas of eastern Oregon. I apologize for giving it short shrift in the initial overview.

I reached Olive Lake by way of the Elkhorn Scenic Drive out of Baker City, but you can also find it from the north by dropping south on I-395 out of Pendleton or from the west via a more circuitous route off of Highway 26 out of Austin. A good map of the state, county, and Forest Service roads in the lonely outposts of Baker and Grant Counties is a wise traveling accessory if you want to be adventurous with peace of mind.

The campground is shaped like a horseshoe around the north end of the lake, offering either lake-front living or views from just about every site. There are a total of 23 tent sites, 21 of which can also be RV sites. Two sites are walk-in only. There are two group sites and three picnic areas. Sites are gargantuan in size and generously spaced, so have no worries about feeling hemmed in. Low-bush undergrowth is spare, which further enhances the feeling of openness. Lodgepole pines, with their slim trunks, don't clutter the camp-

> *Olive Lake benefits from a combination of historical, recreational, and environmental preservation.*

RATINGS

Beauty: ✩ ✩ ✩ ✩
Privacy: ✩ ✩ ✩ ✩
Spaciousness: ✩ ✩ ✩ ✩ ✩
Quiet: ✩ ✩ ✩ ✩ ✩
Security: ✩ ✩ ✩ ✩
Cleanliness: ✩ ✩ ✩ ✩ ✩
Insect control: ✩ ✩ ✩

ADDRESS: Olive Lake
Campground
c/o North Fork John
Day Ranger District
P.O. Box 158
Ukiah, OR 97880

OPERATED BY: Umatilla National
Forest

INFORMATION: (541) 427-3231

OPEN: Late May to October

SITES: 21

EACH SITE HAS: Picnic table, fire grill,
shade trees

ASSIGNMENT: First come,
first served; no reser-
vations

REGISTRATION: Self-registration on
site

FACILITIES: Vault toilets, no
piped water, 2 group
sites, day-use areas

PARKING: At campsites only

FEE: $5

ELEVATION: 6,000 feet

RESTRICTIONS: **Pets:** On leash only
Fires: In fire rings
only
Alcohol: Permitted
Vehicles: 21-foot RV
size limit, no
hookups
Other: Gas and elec-
tric boat motors
allowed

ground yet provide high-canopy relief from the sun on hot days and precipitation on wet ones.

Many of the campers who occupied sites when I visited had a "settled in" look about them suggesting they had been there a long time. Many of these regulars return year after year to their favorite spots and quickly become part of the scenery. According to the camp hosts, the majority of campers who enjoy Olive Lake are repeat customers. Maybe that's why they eyed my car suspiciously when I drove in.

Olive Lake, pitted in its center with an island of trees, sits high in the Greenhorn Range of the Blue Mountains at an elevation of 6,000 feet. The Greenhorn Unit of the North Fork John Day Wilderness can be accessed via a short hike heading southeast from the south end of the lake. The boundary between the Umatilla National Forest and the Malheur National Forest works its way in right angles along high rock buttes and crumbled ridges southwest of the lake. To the north, the largest unit of the North Fork John Day Wilderness encompasses 86,000 acres, creating a protected passageway for the North Fork John Day River and visitors looking to enjoy its Wild & Scenic designation.

Recreationally, the lake is a destination for anglers who are allowed to use boats with both electric and gas motors (strange, so close to a wilderness boundary) to chase after their catch. Kokanee, cutthroat, rainbow, and brook trout are the prime fish to catch. A 2.5-mile trail surrounding the lake is an easy evening stroll, but a longer, more challenging hike takes you north and west to Saddle Camp and Ridge. You can hike along the spine of Saddle Ridge or make the crest of Saddle Camp your turnaround point. A loop hike continues down Saddle Ridge and along Lost Creek at various points to return to Olive Lake either via a trail or FS 10. Half of this loop trip winds through designated wilderness, where you won't encounter any motorized travel.

Historically, Olive Lake was the water source for the Fremont Powerhouse, which served mining and municipal interests for the first half of the twentieth

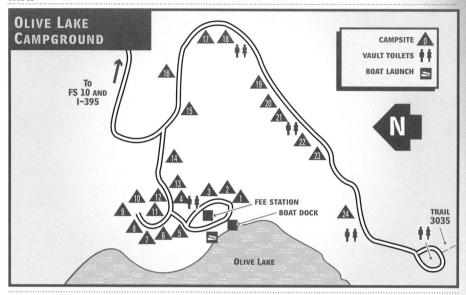

century. A wood-and-steel pipeline was constructed to funnel water nearly straight down the mountainside to the powerhouse. You can still see parts of the pipeline as you travel along FS 10 or along the aforementioned loop hike. The Powerhouse has been placed on the National Register of Historic Places and is open to visitors. The complex includes a caretaker's house and two cabins. The cabins have been refurbished and are now available to rent.

Olive Lake can be busy in the summer, so it's good to have an alternative close by.

GETTING THERE

From Pendleton, drive south on I-395 to the turnoff for FS 10 (approximately 62 miles). Turn left onto FS 10 and drive 26 miles to the campground, which will be on your right.

PAGE SPRINGS CAMPGROUND

> *Of three BLM campgrounds in the Steens Mountain area, Page Springs is the more centrally located for day trips and the only one open year-round.*

ONE LOOK AT THE southeastern expanse of Oregon, roughly 60 miles south of Burns, and you know you're in a place where country-western music is as common as cornbread. Mile after dusty mile, scraggly sagebrush, twisted juniper, and jagged rimrock share a landscape punctuated only by the hulk of mile-high Steens Mountain. This is the highest fault-block mountain in the nation and a snowcapped beacon for all of southeast Oregon.

The region was once the turf of the largest cattle ranch in the United States. Pete French arrived in the Donner und Blitzen River Valley in 1872 with 120 head of cattle and built an empire that totaled 45,000 cattle and 200,000 acres. Cattle operations still exist in parts of the Steens Mountain area today. But with all the natural wonders to behold, outdoor recreation and tourism are emerging as alternatives to traditional sources of income that are gradually fading away.

Page Springs Campground sits invitingly in the midst of this spectrum. Maintained by the Bureau of Land Management out of its Burns district office, Page Springs is one of three public campgrounds that the Bureau provides for visitors. I prefer it because it is centrally located for interesting day trips, which await in just about every direction. It is also the only one of the three campgrounds that is open all year.

Once you've settled in among the sagebrush and aspens, stretch your legs after the hot, dusty drive and explore the immediate surroundings on a 1.8-mile stroll that follows the meandering Donner und Blitzen River through tall stands of surprisingly lush grasses and other hardy indigenous vegetation. This short path is part of a longer route known as the Desert Trail that will, if the efforts of the national Desert Trail Association are successful, provide access to some of the most beautiful arid sections of North America between

RATINGS

Beauty: ✿ ✿ ✿ ✿
Privacy: ✿ ✿ ✿
Spaciousness: ✿ ✿ ✿
Quiet: ✿ ✿ ✿ ✿ ✿
Security: ✿ ✿ ✿ ✿
Cleanliness: ✿ ✿ ✿ ✿ ✿
Insect control: ✿

Canada and Mexico. Oregon's contribution to the trail network is 77 miles.

Now that you're warmed up (or cooled down, more accurately), consider the more distant options. If you're visiting the area in summer, you may want to escape the intense, merciless heat with a drive around Steens Mountain National Backcountry Byway. Be sure to fill your gas tank, and carry extra water for both you and the car. Humans require a gallon per person per day, I've heard; although that doesn't seem quite adequate around here. Better to carry extra than too little. The road to Steens is quite rough, the entire loop distance is 66 miles, and what minimal emergency services exist are in Frenchglen, which will be well behind you once you set out. The weather can change quickly and dramatically, so be prepared for extremes of wind and precipitation. Snow is not uncommon in midsummer at higher altitudes. One last thing: The road is not recommended for RVs. (Isn't that just a beautiful thing?)

While all this emergency preparedness may sound either overly dramatic or a bit daunting, you'll thank me later. Once you reach the summit of Steens, you'll want to stick around a while and take in all that this magnificently desolate area has to offer. And you'll be making numerous stops along the way, as there are overlooks and short hikes to distract you.

Take your time and enjoy the journey. Think about it: When was the last time you had an opportunity to drive to the top of a 9,773-foot mountain that unabashedly bares so many of its geologic secrets? Witness the effects of glacial activity with such clear-cut examples as Kiger, Little Blitzen, Big Indian, and Wild horse Gorges—massive U-shaped troughs up to half a mile deep. The mountain is a veritable living laboratory for botanists and biologists, with five distinct habitat zones ringing its slopes.

Wildlife abounds in the Steens Mountain area, and Malheur National Wildlife Refuge just north of Page Springs provides viewing areas from which as many as 280 species of birds and nearly 60 species of mammals have been observed. The refuge's 185,000 acres of lakes, ponds, marshes, and soggy meadows

KEY INFORMATION

ADDRESS: Page Springs Campground c/o Burns District Office 28910 U.S. Highway 20 West Hines, OR 97738

OPERATED BY: Bureau of Land Management

INFORMATION: (541) 573-4400

OPEN: Year-round

SITES: 31

EACH SITE HAS: Picnic table, fire pit with grill, shade trees

ASSIGNMENT: First come, first served; no reservations

REGISTRATION: Self-registration on site

FACILITIES: Pit toilets, piped water (turned off in winter), garbage service, group picnic shelter; limited disabled access

PARKING: At campsites

FEE: $4

ELEVATION: 4,200 feet

RESTRICTIONS: Pets: On leash only
Fires: In fire pits only
Alcohol: Not permitted
Vehicles: No hookups for RVs or trailers

MAP

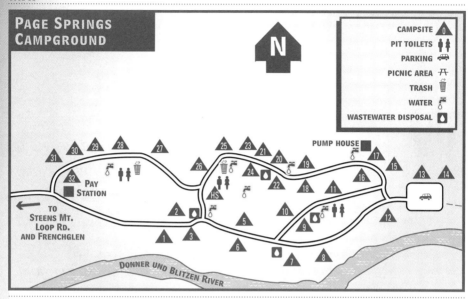

PAGE SPRINGS CAMPGROUND

N

CAMPSITE	⌂
PIT TOILETS	🚹🚺
PARKING	🚗
PICNIC AREA	⛱
TRASH	🗑
WATER	🚰
WASTEWATER DISPOSAL	▣

PUMP HOUSE

PAY STATION

← TO STEENS MT. LOOP RD. AND FRENCHGLEN

HS

DONNER UND BLITZEN RIVER

GETTING THERE

Drive south from just east of Burns on SR 205 about 60 miles to the town of Frenchglen (named in honor of cattle baron Pete French and his equally ambitious father-in-law, Hugh Glenn). Find North Loop Steens Mountain Road, and head east about 4 miles. The campground is adjacent to the oasis-like Donner und Blitzen River.

rank it as one of the top havens for breeding waterfowl, upland game birds, fur-bearers, and big game. Because Page Springs is open all year, bird enthusiasts should try to plan their trips to the refuge anytime from late February through May, when wave after wave of migratory winged creatures take to the skies: tundra swans, Canada geese, lesser sandhill cranes in February; shorebirds such as willets, long-billed curlews, and avocets in April; thousands upon thousands of songbirds in May. Beware, however, of the heavy mosquito population present until midsummer. Herds of the wild Kiger mustang, a direct descendant of the horse introduced to America by Spanish conquistadors, still roam areas around the Steens and are managed by the BLM. A wild horse and burro adoption program is a popular and humane means through which the Burns BLM controls the size of these herds.

SOUTH FORK
CAMPGROUND

WELCOME TO SOUTH FORK, U.S.A. The name of this flick is *From Here to Unity*. This is South Fork Campground of the Wallowa-Whitman National Forest, on the banks of the South Fork Burnt River 7 miles from the intersection of Unity and the rest of the world. If you run into anyone you know out here, you'd better analyze how you're living your life.

My traveling companion and I were doing just that when we found ourselves on the verge of darkness in very unfamiliar territory with a gas gauge registering "Panic very soon." We saw nothing but darkened hills as far as the horizon, and our itinerary dictated we should have been significantly farther east.

A logical person would have taken the first campground they encountered. But that guy had been trouble the whole damn trip, so we dumped him fast and, knowing that dedication applied tonight would avoid crisis tomorrow, we pressed on.

U.S. Highway 26 in this sector of eastern Oregon is one long downgrade followed by a long uphill followed by another long downhill followed by . . . well, you get the picture. In the eternal days of July, when the sun doesn't even think about setting before 9:00 p.m., twilight on a forest-lined freeway can be very dangerous at 70 miles an hour. This is the time of evening when deer decide to cross the road, a fear that prompted me to tail a tractor trailer rather than zipping on ahead. When I saw the sign for Unity, I took my first breath and knew we were in the safety zone. We took the right turn for the South Fork Road and, at the crack of darkness, stumbled blindly into South Fork Campground after a missed turn or two, unloaded the back of the car, climbed in, and went promptly to sleep.

The morning unveiled a camping scene I wasn't quite prepared for; it was, in a word, delightful! Giant

> *You've got to go a long way to find a campground with few people, piped water, excellent scenery, a great trout-fishing stream, and access just off a main highway.*

RATINGS

Beauty: ✪ ✪ ✪
Privacy: ✪ ✪ ✪ ✪ ✪
Spaciousness: ✪ ✪ ✪ ✪ ✪
Quiet: ✪ ✪ ✪ ✪ ✪
Security: ✪
Cleanliness: ✪ ✪
Insect control: ✪ ✪

KEY INFORMATION

ADDRESS: South Fork
Campground
c/o Unity Ranger
District
214 Main Street
Unity, OR 97884

OPERATED BY: Wallowa-Whitman
National Forest

INFORMATION: (541) 446-3351

OPEN: May to October

SITES: 14

EACH SITE HAS: Picnic table, fire
grill; some shade
trees

ASSIGNMENT: First come, first
served; no reserva-
tions

REGISTRATION: Self-registration on
site

FACILITIES: Vault toilets, piped
water

PARKING: At campsites

FEE: None

ELEVATION: 4,400 feet

RESTRICTIONS: Pets: On leash only
Fires: In fire grills
only
Alcohol: Permitted
Vehicles: 28-foot RV
size limit

old Douglas fir stand watch over the gentle glug, glug of the South Fork River. Massive campsites, accessorized with giant fire rings and Paul Bunyan-sized picnic tables, sport that comfortable, lived-in look. Most of the sites are like small homesteading claims, each one abutting the brushy banks of the South Fork Burnt River. Piped water at such a remote location is a major advantage. Make sure you fill all your water bottles if you're planning to be gone for the day.

Recreational opportunities in the summer run the gamut. I was content to sit beside the creek and drink my coffee, trying not to think about the amount of road time that lay ahead. I would have preferred a hike or bike ride. Hiking is a good option in the summer, when you are likely to be quite alone. The crowds arrive later in the fall in the form of hunters, roaming the upper reaches for their quota of elk and deer. For specific destinations, Monument Rock (and its accompanying wilderness), Table Rock, and Bull Run Rock are the most notable land formations near South Fork and are accessible via trailheads further along FS 600.

Bird watching can be an enjoyable pastime in the South Fork Burnt Basin, with more than seventy species identified. I guess you could say that the South Fork Burnt River is, to some degree, for the birds!

Be aware that out in this part of eastern Oregon, not unlike other cattle-dependent areas in Oregon, the cows graze freely and boundaries between private property, forest lands, and wilderness areas mean nothing to them. As a result, they sometimes trample fragile alpine environments, whereas you might be reprimanded for doing the same, and the waters that flow through the landscape aren't necessarily pristine.

This doesn't excuse those of us with more developed brains from leaving the land as we found it and adhering to the "pack it in, pack it out" credo just as much as we would elsewhere. Don't do as the cows do, do as the signs say. And don't forget to support the local economy—and quite possibly save yourself a headache—by filling up your gas tank in Unity.

MAP

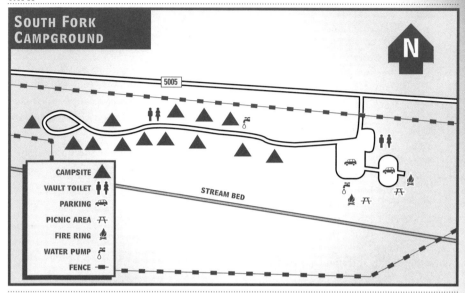

GETTING THERE

From US 26 in Unity, turn right onto South Fork Burnt River Road and drive 6 miles to the campground.

STRAWBERRY CAMPGROUND

> *Strawberry is a strategically placed, cool wayside stopover when traveling on US 26 through the broad, fascinating plain of the Upper John Day River.*

SUMMER TRAVEL IN and around the historic burgs of Prairie City, John Day, Mount Vernon, Dayville, and Austin is marked by intensely hot days that can sap the strength and resolve of even the hardiest road warrior. If you are about to reach the wilting stage when passing through Prairie City, turn south onto Bridge Street, cross the John Day River, and follow Strawberry Road to its end. Your reward is a cool haven in Malheur National Forest high above the valley floor.

Although there is nothing in any park literature explaining the extensive use of the word strawberry throughout the immediate vicinity, someone must know why this area was so labeled. The best I can guess is that a sunset captured someone's imagination, or there was a settler named Strawberry. If anyone has the answer, let me know.

At any rate, at Strawberry Campground at the end of Strawberry Road, Strawberry Creek rumbles off of Strawberry Mountain, which is the high point (9,038 feet) of the Strawberry Range and constitutes the focal point of the Strawberry Mountain Wilderness. Oh, yes, there's Strawberry Lake, too. At least it's easy to remember the names of things around here. There's also Strawberry Falls, and I'm sure it's only a matter of time before someone dubs Strawberry Spring!

The drive up to the campground rises gradually through the grassy meadows of private ranchlands and then turns immediately uphill for a gutsy, gravelly climb in the last few miles. As you enter the campground, cross Strawberry Creek to find yourself in a pleasant little forested park hugging the hillside.

The campground is shaped in a near-perfect circle and follows the natural contours of the hillside, with some sites on higher ground, some recessed from the camp road, and some nestled in little glens. It's hard to

RATINGS

Beauty: ✿ ✿ ✿ ✿
Privacy: ✿ ✿ ✿ ✿
Spaciousness: ✿ ✿ ✿ ✿
Quiet: ✿ ✿ ✿ ✿ ✿
Security: ✿ ✿ ✿
Cleanliness: ✿ ✿ ✿
Insect control: ✿ ✿ ✿

name the better sites, as most are visible to each other. I suppose the sites on the outer arc of the circle afford the most privacy. When I was there, it seemed as though the inner circle of sites was in the process of creating a true inner circle as an afternoon sing-along (a.k.a. party), complete with guitar strumming, shaped up. This might be commonplace given the generally friendly camping atmosphere at Strawberry.

Strawberry Campground is a logical base for some good hiking in the Strawberry Mountain Wilderness, but the elevation gains coming in from the north can be abrupt. A popular route is the Strawberry Basin Trail, which leads to a vista below the summit of Strawberry Mountain. The rise is moderate and the one-way mileage is just over 5, with stops at Strawberry Lake and Strawberry Falls at roughly the 1- and 2-mile marks, respectively. These make for good, short outbound destinations to test the limbs and get the muscles warmed.

Other hiking options await in the Aldrich Mountains to the west and at Lookout Mountain to the east. Access to these two areas requires driving part (or all, if time allows) of the scenic loop that encircles the compact Strawberry Mountain Wilderness. The route is an easy 75 miles, linking two state highways, forest service roads, and a county road—paved the entire way—for a 360-degree view of Grant County's tallest peak and the surrounding environs. Some of the easiest hiking access to Strawberry Mountain's summit is from the south up through Logan Valley. Forest Road 1640 takes you to trailheads that begin deep in a narrow notch between wilderness boundaries, thus putting you within a reasonably short and gradual ascent to the top.

While the pioneers who first made their way into the Upper John Day Basin are long gone, a proud heritage is strongly evident today in the number of historical societies, museums, and markers that preserve the colorful past shaped mainly by the gold mining, ranching, lumbering, and transportation industries. If you're as interested as I am in the human activities that shaped the many fascinating regions of Oregon, take time to visit places such as the Kam Wah Chung & Co. Museum in John Day or the Dewitt Museum in Prairie

KEY INFORMATION

ADDRESS: Strawberry Campground c/o Prairie City Ranger District P.O. Box 337 Prairie City, OR 97759

OPERATED BY: Malheur National Forest

INFORMATION: (541) 820-3311

OPEN: Late May through October

SITES: 11

EACH SITE HAS: Picnic table, fire grill, shade trees

ASSIGNMENT: First come, first served; no reservations

REGISTRATION: Self-registration on site

FACILITIES: Vault toilets, piped water

PARKING: At campsites

FEE: $6

ELEVATION: 5,700 feet

RESTRICTIONS: Pets: On leash only
Fires: In fire pits only
Alcohol: Permitted
Vehicles: RVs and trailers not recommended, no hookups

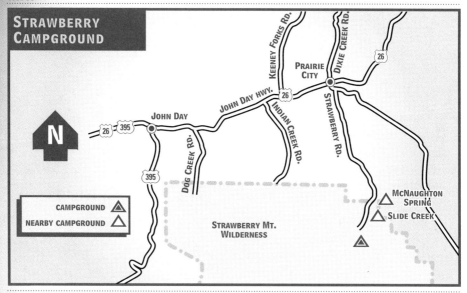

STRAWBERRY CAMPGROUND

GETTING THERE

From Prairie City, drive south on Strawberry Road for 11 miles to the campground at the road's end. The last several miles climb very steeply and are not recommended for trailers or RVs.

City. Much can be learned from the artifacts, memorabilia, and photographs on display.

For a taste of a real working ranch, stop in at Oxbow Ranch on Strawberry Road. The 7,000-square-foot remodeled ranch house operates as a bed-and-breakfast with beautifully appointed guest rooms. For guests of the ranch or out-of-towners passing through, trail-riding and carriage tours are also available (for a fee).

One final note: Portions of the Malheur National Forest were ravaged by wildfires in 2002 and are currently undergoing restoration efforts. These efforts can take many years, so check with the proper ranger district office for the most updated information that may affect your recreational plans.

TWO PAN CAMPGROUND

Lostine

TUCKED AWAY IN THE far northeastern corner of Oregon on a broad, grassy plain that once was the beloved homeland of the proud Nez Perce Indians sits a magical little kingdom of imposing granite peaks, flower-choked meadows, rushing glacial creeks, and crystalline alpine air.

Eagle Cap Wilderness, rising high above the Wallowa Valley in the Wallowa Mountains, is regularly referred to as "America's Little Switzerland" and even sports a Matterhorn of its own. Various sources list the peak's elevation anywhere between 9,832 feet and 10,004 feet (about 5,000 feet shorter than its European counterpart). Depending on whose measurement you trust, the Matterhorn might be the highest point in Eagle Cap.

Following close on its heels, however, are several dozen peaks above 8,000 feet. In fact, Oregon has 29 peaks that are 9,000 feet or higher. Seventeen of them are clustered in Eagle Cap, the largest wilderness tract in Oregon at more than 350,000 acres.

Two Pan Campground may not win any beauty awards. But whoever said a frog that doesn't want to be a prince has no rightful place in the universe? Two Pan is conveniently situated at the intersection of road's end and trail's start, which makes it an ideal base camp for exploring the aforementioned magic kingdom.

The road to Two Pan, however, follows the Wild and Scenic Lostine River south and offers the beauty that is perhaps less evident at Two Pan, piercing deep into the Wallowa range and gaining altitude steadily once it enters the canyon. The drive up from the valley floor and into the canyon is an education in both the geology and history of the area. About a million years ago, a large glacier carved out the Lostine River Canyon as it advanced down from the center of the Wallowa Mountains. Grass-covered mounds in the

> *Two Pan Campground affords one of the best jumping-off spots for extended backpacking in "America's Little Switzerland."*

RATINGS

Beauty: ✿ ✿ ✿ ✿ ✿
Privacy: ✿ ✿ ✿
Spaciousness: ✿ ✿ ✿ ✿
Quiet: ✿ ✿ ✿ ✿ ✿
Security: ✿ ✿ ✿ ✿
Cleanliness: ✿ ✿ ✿ ✿ ✿
Insect control: ✿ ✿ (summer)
    ✿ ✿ ✿ ✿ (off-season)

KEY INFORMATION

ADDRESS: Two Pan
Campground
c/o Eagle Cap
Ranger District
P.O. Box 907
Baker, OR 97814

OPERATED BY: Wallowa-Whitman
National Forest

INFORMATION: (541) 523-1205 or
(541) 426-5546 (Wallowa Mountains Visitors Center)

OPEN: Mid-June to
November

SITES: 6

EACH SITE HAS: Picnic table, fire grill

ASSIGNMENT: First come, first
served; no reservations

REGISTRATION: Not necessary

FACILITIES: Vault toilets, no
piped water; stock
watering tank and
hitch rack

PARKING: In campground

FEE: None

ELEVATION: 5,600 feet

RESTRICTIONS: Pets: On leash only
Fires: In fire pits
only
Alcohol: Permitted
Vehicles: No RV or
trailer accommodations

lowlands, known as moraines, are rock and soil deposits left by the glacier in its advance-and-melt periods over hundreds of years. Based on the height of the moraines, geologists estimate that ice as thick as 400 feet once covered this area.

Pole Bridge Picnic Area (a bit past the national forest boundary) is the site of an old bridge, constructed entirely of poles, that once crossed the river here. About all that's left is a piece of foundation, but it's a nice excuse to stop. Fortify yourself for the remainder of the drive with a snack as you examine further evidence of glacial activity in the deep gorge that the river has cut into the canyon. This is about half a mile up the road from the picnic grounds.

Two miles farther is an even better opportunity to view the natural beauty of the Wild and Scenic Lostine River. A short trail takes you to an overlook of Lostine Gorge, a dramatic plunge between steep canyon walls where vegetation works hard to survive amid the predominant rocks and boulders.

The Wallowa Mountains were once the site of busy gold and silver mining. The ramshackle remains of cabins and outbuildings on the privately held Lapover Ranch (at mile 16) are all that remains of mining claims established by settlers from Kansas in 1911. They got in just under the wire—the Wallowa National Forest received its federal designation later that same year. Until Lostine Road was completed to its current end at Two Pan in 1955, the canyon was a popular route for sheepherders moving their flocks to and from the alpine meadows. Apparently, that is how Two Pan got its name—at some point in all their comings and goings, sheepherders passing through left two frying pans hanging from a tree. Okay, not the juiciest story, but facts are facts!

When out sightseeing, you'll be tempted to drink straight from the cold, gushing Lostine to quench your thirst. Hold that thought and keep in mind that the Eagle Cap Wilderness is full of mountain goats, bighorn sheep, elk, deer, and a variety of smaller wild animals. This dramatically increases the risk of giardiasis (a.k.a. diarrhea). Better to boil or treat the glacial flow, unfortunate as that may seem.

MAP

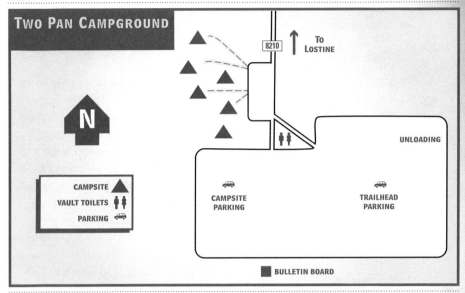

TWO PAN CAMPGROUND

8210 → To LOSTINE

UNLOADING

N

CAMPSITE ▲
VAULT TOILETS 🚹🚺
PARKING 🚗

CAMPSITE
PARKING

TRAILHEAD
PARKING

■ BULLETIN BOARD

If you want seclusion on your exploration of Eagle Cap Wilderness, avoid the Lakes Basin region, which gets overrun by the crowds from Wallowa Lake. If you want to avoid the mosquitoes and biting flies (which are as thick as the crowds in midsummer), go in September. If you want to treat yourself after roughing it in the wilds, stop in at Wallowa Lake Lodge (on the south shore at the end of SR 82). This fine old resort offers pleasant rooms, fine dining, and lively banter with the friendly staff.

GETTING THERE

To reach Two Pan from Lostine (10 miles west of Enterprise on SR 82), follow Lostine River Road due south all the way to its end at the campground (18 miles). Lostine River Road becomes FS 8210 at the national forest boundary, about halfway to the campground.

WALLOWA LAKE STATE PARK CAMPGROUND

> *Wallowa Lake is the gateway to the Eagle Cap Wilderness and Hell's Canyon area.*

THIS IS THE BIG TAMALE of Oregon Campgrounds. It's not really the campground itself that is noteworthy but its impressive neighbors, which set Wallowa Lake State Park apart and make this area a must-visit place. For starters, Wallowa Lake itself is popular for boating and fishing. Word to the wise: Bring your camera along to snap shots of the sparkling lake surrounded by the snow-capped mountain peaks.

The Wallowa (pronounced Wa-LA-wa) area is also renowned as the entrance point for popular hiking trails and perhaps one of the area's best backpacking trails: the Lakes Basin Trail, where alpine lakes reflect an up-close view of the 10,000-foot peaks of Eagle Cap Wilderness. Simply the drive in will take your breath away as you encounter what are known as the Alps of Oregon. Not to be outdone, Hell's Canyon on the Oregon–Idaho border a short 30-minute drive away is the deepest gorge in North America, at one mile, and is a popular whitewater-rafting destination.

But you don't need to travel far to see any action: it seems like everything you could possibly want is in this area (including a wedding chapel!). Guided horseback tours, canoeing, restaurants, even bumper cars and a mini-golf course are among the offerings.

You can also ride a tramway to the top of 8,200-foot Mount Howard, with views of Wallowa Lake and the Eagle Cap Wilderness. Board the tram at quaint Wallowa Lake Village, a town designed to resemble those you might ramble through in the Swiss Alps (it bills itself as "The Switzerland of America").

The little town of Joseph nearby is worth a trip just to see, with local artist galleries and shops lining the main drag. In a world of overdeveloped mountain towns, Joseph is a refreshing blend of modernity that still manages to maintain its authenticity. All of this

RATINGS

Beauty: ✩ ✩ ✩ ✩ ✩
Privacy: ✩ ✩
Spaciousness: ✩ ✩ ✩
Quiet: ✩ ✩
Security: ✩ ✩ ✩
Cleanliness: ✩ ✩ ✩
Insect control: ✩ ✩ ✩

means one thing, though: it can get packed, especially on a holiday weekend. (Trust me: You shouldn't even think about showing up without reservations in hand on a long summer weekend unless you want the campground entrance staff to snicker at you).

Besides the campground's 89 tent-only sites, the park offers 121 full-hookup sites, two wooden yurts, and one deluxe two-story cabin.

Bird-watching enthusiasts enjoy Wallowa Lake State Park for the abundance of feathered species that enjoy this lovely land, including pheasants, quail, hummingbirds, and the rarely spotted belted kingfisher. Some of the better birding areas nearby the park include the Chief Joseph Mountain trail and Old Chief Joseph's gravesite.

Guided hunting trips are also popular here; those with the proper permits can pull in big game such as elk, bears, cougars, and even big-horn sheep.

The park offers two picnic areas, a marina, and a boat launch. For those in the mood to test the water, but not necessarily looking to plunge in, try parasailing, offered from May to September. Purchase tickets at the Eagle Cap Packstation.

The Wallowa Lake Highway Forest State Scenic Corridor, a day-use site located along the Wallowa River, is a popular fishing and wildlife-viewing area. Steelhead fishing is popular during the spring and fall. The canyon rises steeply on both sides of the road, and you can almost expect to see te deer, elk, and bear that live here. Flowers blanket the area in the spring.

If you come at the end of September, you'll enjoy joining the locals at the town's annual Alpenfest fair, a Swiss-Bavarian festival that has been staged in the traditional Oktoberfest style every autumn since 1974.

If you're looking for a place to bring a group with varied interests—and particularly if you can manage to get away when it's not one of the summer holiday weekends—you can't go wrong with this fascinating area.

KEY INFORMATION

ADDRESS: Wallowa Lake State Park
72214 Marina Lane
Joseph, OR 97846

OPERATED BY: Oregon State Parks

INFORMATION: (541) 432-4185, (800) 452-5687; www.oregon stateparks.org

OPEN: Year-round

SITES: 89 tent sites

EACH SITE HAS: Picnic table, fire ring

ASSIGNMENT: First-come, first-served or by reservation at (800) 452-5687 or www.reserve america.com ($6 fee)

REGISTRATION: At campground entrance

FACILITIES: Flush toilets, hot showers, laundry, firewood

PARKING: At park entrance and at individual sites

FEE: $13 October–April, $17 May–September; $7 per additional vehicle

ELEVATION: 4,450 feet

RESTRICTIONS: Pets: On leash only
Fires: In fire rings only
Alcohol: Permitted at campsites only
Vehicles: RVs and trailers allowed

MAP

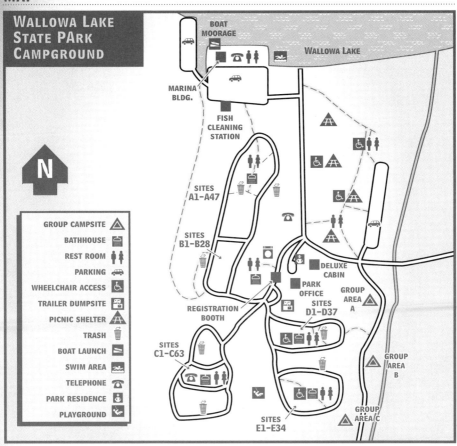

WALLOWA LAKE STATE PARK CAMPGROUND

BOAT MOORAGE

WALLOWA LAKE

MARINA BLDG.

FISH CLEANING STATION

N

SITES A1–A47

SITES B1–B28

DELUXE CABIN

GROUP AREA A

PARK OFFICE

SITES D1–D37

GROUP CAMPSITE	
BATHHOUSE	
REST ROOM	
PARKING	
WHEELCHAIR ACCESS	
TRAILER DUMPSITE	
PICNIC SHELTER	
TRASH	
BOAT LAUNCH	
SWIM AREA	
TELEPHONE	
PARK RESIDENCE	
PLAYGROUND	

REGISTRATION BOOTH

SITES C1–C63

GROUP AREA B

GROUP AREA C

SITES E1–E34

GETTING THERE

From Enterprise (east of LaGrande), drive 12.4 miles south on OR 82 (passing through Joseph) to Wallowa Lake State Park. Continue past Wallowa Lake and turn right into the campground.

APPENDICES AND **INDEX**

APPENDIX A
CAMPING EQUIPMENT
CHECKLIST

Except for the large and bulky items on this list, I keep a plastic storage container full of the essentials for car camping so they're ready to go when I am. I make a last-minute check of the inventory, resupply anything that's low or missing, and away I go.

COOKING UTENSILS
Bottle opener
Bottles of salt, pepper, spices, sugar, and cooking oil and maple syrup in water-proof, spillproof containers
Can opener
Corkscrew
Cups, plastic or tin
Dish soap (biodegradable), sponge and towel
Flatware
Food of your choice
Frying pan, spatula
Fuel for stove
Lighter, matches in waterproof container
Plates
Pocketknife
Fire starter
Pot with lid
Stove
Tin foil
Wooden spoon

FIRST-AID KIT
Aspirin
Band-Aids
First-aid cream
Gauze pads
Insect repellent
Moleskin
Sunscreen/lip balm
Tape, waterproof adhesive

SLEEPING GEAR
Pillow
Sleeping bag
Sleeping pad, inflatable or insulated
Tent with ground tarp and rainfly

MISCELLANEOUS
Bath soap (biodegradable), washcloth and towel
Camp chair
Candles
Cooler
Deck of cards
Flashlight/headlamp
Paper towels
Plastic zip-top bags
Sunglasses
Toilet paper
Water bottle
Wool blanket

OPTIONAL
Barbecue grill
Binoculars
Field guides on bird, plant, and wildlife identification
Fishing rod and tackle
Lantern
Maps (road, trail, topographic, etc.)

APPENDIX B
SOURCES OF
INFORMATION

AAA AUTOMOBILE CLUB OF OREGON
600 SW Market
Portland, OR 97201
(503) 222-6700
www.aaa.com

BUREAU OF LAND MANAGEMENT
P.O. Box 2965, Portland, OR 97232
1515 SW 5th Avenue, Portland, OR 97201
(503) 952-6001
www.or.blm.gov

CRATER LAKE NATIONAL PARK (NPS)
P.O. Box 7
Crater Lake, OR 97604
(541) 594-2211
www.nps.gov/crla

**HELLS CANYON NATIONAL RECREATION
  AREA (USFS)**
P.O. Box 490
Enterprise, OR 97828
(541) 426-4978

**THE MAZAMAS (HIKING AND
  CLIMBING CLUB)**
909 NW 19th Street
Portland, OR 97209
(503) 227-2345

**NATURE OF THE NORTHWEST
  (MAPS AND FIELD GUIDES)**
800 NE Oregon, #5
Portland, OR 97232
(503) 731-4444
www.naturenw.org

OREGON COAST VISITORS ASSOCIATION
P.O. Box 670
Newport, OR 97365
(541) 574-2679 or (888) 628-2101
www.oregon-coast.org

OREGON DEPARTMENT OF FISH AND WILDLIFE
P.O. Box 59
Portland, OR 97207
(503) 229-5410

OREGON TOURISM COMMISSION
775 Summer Street NE
Salem, OR 97310
(800) 547-7842 (toll free nationwide)
www.traveloregon.com

OREGON STATE PARKS AND RECREATION
1115 Commercial Street NE
Salem, OR 97301
(503) 378-8605
www.prd.state.or.us

**OUTDOOR RECREATION INFORMATION CENTER
  (NPS AND USFS INFO FOR THE NORTHWEST)**
222 Yale North (inside REI)
Seattle, WA 98109-5429
(206) 220-7450

RESERVATIONS NORTHWEST
P.O. Box 500
Portland, OR 97207-0500
(503) 731-3411 (800) 452-5687
www.prd.state.or.us/reservation.html

APPENDIX B
SOURCES OF
INFORMATION (continued)

U.S. FISH AND WILDLIFE SERVICE
  (OREGON OFFICE)
P.O. Box 111
Lakeview, OR 97630
(541) 947-3315

U.S. FOREST SERVICE (PACIFIC NORTHWEST
  REGIONAL HEADQUARTERS)
P.O. Box 3623, Portland, OR 97208
333 SW 1st Avenue, Portland, OR 97204
(503) 221-2877
www.fs.fed.us/r6

INDEX

A

Alcohol restrictions. see Key Information
for each campground
Alder Glen Campground, 14–16
Allen Springs campground, 85
Allingham campground, 85
Alsea River, 26, 39
Angling. *See* Fishing
Animals. see Wildlife
Anthony Lakes Recreation Area, 130–32
Attractions
Breitenbush Hot Springs, 57
Corvallis Arts Center, 41
Oregon Coast Aquarium, 9
Stellar Sea Lion Caves, 31
wild mushrooms, 25
See also Events and festivals; Historic
sites; Sites of interest

B

Badger Lake Campground, 44–46
Beachcombing, 18
Beaches. see Coastal campgrounds; Swim-
ming
Beavertail Campground, 47–49
Beverly Beach State Park, 8–10
Big Bend campground, 79–80
Biking
Cape Blanco State Park, 29
Cape Lookout State Park, 11–13
Crater Lake National Park, 111
Jubilee Lake, 143
Metolius River, 86
Mount Thielsen, 123
Siskiyou National Forest, 37
Siuslaw National Forest, 41
Williamette and Marys River, 41
Williamette National Forest, 119–20
Birdwatching
Badger Creek Wilderness, 45
Cape Blanco State Park, 28
Cape Lookout State Park, 11–12

Jubilee Lake, 142
Malheur National Wildlife Refuge,
152–53
Mallard Marsh, 83
Oregon Dunes National Recreation
Area, 34
South Fork Campground, 155
Boating
Alsea River, 25–26
Anthony Lake, 131
Badger Lake, 46
Detroit Lake, 62
Fourmile Lake, 104–06
Hosmer Lake, 82–84
Jubilee Lake, 144
McKenzie River, 91–93
Metolius River, 87
Nestucca River
New River, 28
North Umpqua River, 123
Olive Lake, 149
Oxbow Regional Park, 66
Quartzville Corridor, 100–102
Rogue River, 36–37, 113
Sixes River, 29
Wallowa Lake State Park, 163–65
See also Canoeing; Rafting
Bonneville Dam, 53–55
Bridal Veil Falls, 55
Buckhorn Campground, 133–35
Bureau of Land Management (BLM), 169
Beavertail Campground, 47–49
Elkhorn Valley Campground, 59–61
horse and burro adoption program, 153
Lower Palisades Campground, 79–81
Nestucca River campgrounds, 14–16
Page Springs Campground, 151–53
Yellowbottom Campground, 100–102

C

Camp Creek Campground, 50–52
Camp Sherman, 85, 87

THE BEST
IN TENT
CAMPING
OREGON